FIGS. 1— 4 MISSEL THRUSH.
    5— 9 SONG THRUSH.
    10—17 BLACKBIRD.

FIGS. 18—19 RING OUZEL.
        20 WHEATEAR.
    21—22 WHINCHAT.
        23 STONECHAT.

FIGS.   24 REDSTART
    25—28 REDBREAST
    29—31 NIGHTINGALE.

THE ROBIN:
A BIOGRAPHY

THE ROBIN:
A BIOGRAPHY

A Year in the Life of Britain's Favourite Bird

STEPHEN MOSS

3 5 7 9 10 8 6 4

Square Peg, an imprint of Vintage,
20 Vauxhall Bridge Road,
London SW1V 2SA

Square Peg is part of the Penguin Random House group of companies whose
addresses can be found at global.penguinrandomhouse.com.

Penguin
Random House
UK

First published by Square Peg in 2017

Penguin.co.uk/vintage

A CIP catalogue record for this book is available from the British Library

ISBN 9781910931318

Typeset in India by Integra Software Services Pvt. Ltd, Pondicherry

Printed and bound in Italy by L.E.G.O. S.p.A.

Penguin Random House is committed to a sustainable future for our
business, our readers and our planet. This book is made from
Forest Stewardship Council® certified paper.

To Sally Rose, my aunt, and June Dolan, my mother-in-law,
who love their garden robins

I have heard of a closet naturalist who, slighting
the labours of a brother in the field, alleged that
he could pen a volume on the robin; but surely,
if confined to the subject and without the aid
of fable, it would prove a duller book than
Robinson Crusoe.

William MacGillivray

Art thou the bird whom Man loves best,
The pious bird with the scarlet breast,
Our little English Robin...

William Wordsworth,
'The Redbreast Chasing the Butterfly', 1806

BRITAIN'S FAVOURITE BIRD

As I write these words, a little bird comes to the open door of my back-garden office. Hopping towards me, he cocks his head to one side as if checking me out. Then he flies up into a nearby elder and, moments later, begins to pour out his delicate, tuneful song, full of nuance and pathos. On this late-autumn afternoon, when all is quiet in the natural world, this sight and sound fills me with an unexpected rush of joy and delight.

The bird is, of course, a robin – how could it be anything else? No other bird is quite so confident or approachable; and no other species sings so regularly at this time of year, as the nights are rapidly drawing in, and we prepare for the winter season to come.

From deep in our childhood memories, we recall the robin's image on a million Christmas cards: the pert, plump, red-breasted bird that is as much a part of the festive season as mince pies or presents piled up beneath the tree. Now, and indeed throughout the winter, the robin is a constant presence outside our kitchen window, inclining its head to one side as if nagging us to restock the bird table, to make sure it gets enough to eat.

Whatever the time of year, we welcome robins into our lives. Robins are one of the first birds to begin singing each year – in my Somerset garden they often start as early as New Year's Day. Spring may still be several months away, but those brief, measured phrases, methodically laid down upon the winter air like musical notes along a stave, herald the season to come.

By March or April, the robins in my garden have staked out their territories. At this time of year, whenever I leave the house, I can hear three or four birds, each delivering their song almost continuously from dawn to dusk. I know that they do so for purely biological reasons – to repel rival males and to attract a mate – but I defy anyone to hear a singing robin and not carry on with a spring in their step. Sometimes biology must give way to emotion.

Soon afterwards, each pair gets down to the serious business of raising a family: building a nest, laying a clutch of eggs and, when these hatch, flying to and fro to find food for their brood of hungry chicks. If they manage to fledge their offspring – and with their exposed, open nest robins often fall victim to predatory magpies or jays – then sometime in June I shall have a new visitor outside my office door. A juvenile robin: a speckled, brownish creature, whose plump body and black, beady eyes are the only clues to its parentage.

Around this time the adults stop singing for a few weeks, hiding away deep inside the hawthorn bushes and cider-apple trees to moult their worn plumage into a set of spanking new feathers. Then, towards the end of the summer holidays, they start to sing again – having, uniquely amongst British birds, established an autumn and winter territory. And so, as the year ends, my robin continues to serenade me as I go about my daily chores.

I say *my* robin, but the chances are this is not the bird I heard singing back on New Year's Day. Robins rarely live longer than a year or two, and so this songster is quite likely to be the son of that original bird, or perhaps an interloper from another garden nearby.

My aunt, who has fed robins in the same Sussex garden for almost sixty years, dismisses this notion as 'stuff and nonsense'. She claims that the same bird has been coming to her window ledge for at least ten years, and no amount of urging on my part will convince her otherwise. Nor am I allowed to mention that other inconvenient truth about robins: that of all our garden birds, they are the most aggressive and violent, sometimes fighting rival males to the death. Like other devotees of the robin, she hears this, but resolutely chooses to ignore it.

Alongside the real, biological robin, there's also a cultural and historical 'robin'. This other aspect of the robin is expressed through poetry and prose, and in our hearts, as we admire, love and celebrate the wonder of this little bird.

Robins are embedded in our literary culture – arguably even more so than those other classic avian icons, the skylark and the nightingale. In Andrew Lack's delightful book *Redbreast* (published in 2008, as an updating of his father David's 1950 volume *Robin Redbreast*), the index lists the various authors who have included the robin in their poetry or prose.

This includes those you would expect – Chaucer and Shakespeare – together with novelists Anne and Emily (but not Charlotte) Brontë, Anthony Trollope, George Eliot and D.H. Lawrence. Other writers who have included robins in their prose or poetry include Robert Herrick and Robert Burns, William Blake and William Wordsworth, a quartet of Johns – Clare, Keats, Bunyan and Betjeman – Alfred, Lord Tennyson and Samuel Taylor Coleridge, W.H. Auden and Ted Hughes, Edward Thomas and Thomas Hardy,

Sir Walter Scott and Robert Louis Stevenson, and children's authors Frances Hodgson Burnett and Enid Blyton.

Yet even though the robin is a popular subject for poets, as Richard Mabey points out in his introduction to *Redbreast*, it rarely reaches the literary heights of other species: 'There are no truly great robin poems, like Ted Hughes's "Swifts" or George Meredith's "The Lark Ascending"; the robin simply isn't that kind of heroic, elusive creature.'

We love the robin for its no-nonsense familiarity, its ordinariness, and its approachability. Gardeners have long regarded the robin as a friendly companion, perching on a garden spade, and waiting expectantly for the soil to be overturned so it can grab a juicy earthworm.

Its neighbourliness allows us to at least begin to imagine what life must be like for this little bird; for it haunts exactly the same sphere as us. It remains mostly on or near the ground, not rising high into the heavens like a skylark; and also spends the whole year with us, not gallivanting off to some distant, unknown continent, like the swift.

The cultural aspect of robins is not always entirely positive: they may bring darkness as well as light. If one dares to venture across the threshold and into our home, or flies in through an open window, there is a longstanding superstition that someone in that household is doomed to die. Yet even as bad omens, we make them part of our myths and stories.

Robins have long been regarded as religious symbols: according to Christian mythology, the red breast is supposed to symbolise the blood of Christ, the feathers having been stained as the bird pulled out spurs from his crown of thorns. And no account of the cultural importance of robins could fail to recognise their central place in the festive season. But the reason robins are so ubiquitous on Christmas cards may come as a surprise, as we shall discover in Chapter 12.

* * * * * *

The cultural, literary and historical robin is, of course, an entirely human invention, but no less real for that. Indeed, if this aspect of the robin didn't exist – if it were just another anonymous species of chat, like most of the other 300 members of the avian family it belongs to – then it would hardly merit the attention it gets. For no other species has quite so great a hold on our national psyche.

So I wasn't at all surprised when in May 2015 the robin topped the poll for Britain's Favourite Bird. The only real question was by how big a margin it would win. In the event, the robin triumphed by a huge distance: of almost a quarter of a million votes cast on the shortlist of ten species it attracted more than a third. The nearest challengers, the barn owl and the blackbird, scored barely a third of the robin's total.

This wasn't the first time the robin had hit the headlines. Back in 1960, *The Times* newspaper had carried out its own (albeit self-selected) poll amongst its readers, in which the robin comfortably beat the red grouse to be crowned Britain's (unofficial) national bird.

The man behind the 2015 poll, David Lindo – aka The Urban Birder – had in the final days of the vote actually lobbied against the robin, coming out openly for his own favourite, the blackbird. But after the result, he hailed the robin's victory with good grace, cleverly linking the bird's less-than-wholesome qualities with aspects of the British national character: 'Despite being a seemingly friendly bird, the robin is hugely territorial and very defensive of its territory. I presume that reflects us as an island nation – that we will stand our ground.'

Maybe he's right – we love the robin because it reminds us of ourselves, with all our faults as well as our virtues. We simply choose to sweep the robin's less savoury qualities under the carpet, and focus instead on its friendly character, its neighbourliness, and its conviviality – all qualities we would like to have. How else can we explain why the robin is so popular?

This may, of course, simply be down to its ubiquity: with more than six million breeding pairs, the robin is second only to the wren as Britain's commonest bird. But it is more likely to be the way the robin lives its whole life alongside us, ever-present during every month and season of the year. Certainly no other British bird is quite so familiar. Wherever I travel in Britain – apart from a few remote offshore islands – I come across robins. In the heart of the city and in the open countryside, while waiting for a train or sitting in my garden, in winter and summer, and by day or by night, I have seen or heard robins: either hopping about in front of me or singing that plaintive, delicate song.

And yet... how much do we *really* know about the robin? Where else in the world can they be found? Why *are* male robins so violent? And, given that until the mid-twentieth century its official name was 'Redbreast', how on earth did the robin get its name? They are just some of the questions I hope to answer in this book...

January

1

A Bright New Year

Robin on a leafless bough,
  Lord in Heaven, how he sings!
Now cold winter's cruel wind
  Makes playmates of withered things...

W.H. Davies, 'Robin Redbreast', 1908

JANUARY

New Year's Day has dawned cold and clear in deepest Somerset, with a thin layer of hoar frost on every twig and branch, and a pleasing crispness underfoot. The mercury remains well below zero, and yet, even before the sun has risen, a small, plump bird is already up and about. Fluffing out his feathers to keep as warm as possible, he turns to reveal an unexpected splash of colour in this otherwise monochrome landscape.

With short, jerky movements, the bird makes his way across the icing-sugared lawn, then hops up onto a low bush and delivers a brief burst of song. Puffs of smoky breath emerge from his half-opened bill, as the notes pierce the chill, silent air. We humans love to hear this sound, but that's not the reason this bird is singing. For this is a male robin, and he's defending his winter territory.

Like all birds – indeed, like every other living thing, including us – this robin is only here because his parents, grandparents, great-grandparents, and so on for countless generations back in time, managed to successfully reproduce.

Now it's his turn to begin that process all over again. The year has only just begun, and spring is still very far away, but this primal impulse is already driving this robin. All his instincts, honed over the 50 million years since songbirds first appeared on Earth, compel him to get the breeding cycle underway. He now needs to choose a territory, defend it against rivals, find and court a mate, fertilise her eggs, build a nest, and feed their chicks until they too are independent, some six or seven months hence.

Think of this robin as a small, colourful ball of feathers with just one aim in life: to breed. If he succeeds, he will pass on his unique genetic heritage to the next and future generations. If he fails, then his chance is gone forever. It's a heavy responsibility; one belied by that sweet, tuneful, delicate song.

Yet, soon after the end of the breeding season, this robin may well be dead. Robins – like most small birds – live their life on a very different timescale to us. They rarely survive for more than two years, and any individual robin has a greater than even chance of dying before it reaches its first birthday. But if he can successfully raise a family, he will have done his duty, and given himself a glimpse of immortality.

At present, though, there is little time for song. On a freezing January day, with only a few short hours of daylight, his first priority must be to find food. Cold weather doesn't kill birds – at least not directly – but the frost and ice that come with it do, by covering up their food, and making it harder to find.

Like most small birds, robins must find and eat between one quarter and one third of their body weight in food – every single day. Fail to do so, and they will die. So the robin stops singing, drops to the ground, and hops across the frosted lawn in search of something to eat.

What exactly *is* a robin? For a simple description, it is hard to beat that written by the greatest of all robin scientists, David Lack, whose 1943 book *The Life of the Robin* remains one of the all-time classics of natural history writing:

> The English [*sic*] robin is a bird rather smaller than a sparrow, in build between a thrush and a warbler, uniform brown on the upperparts, with an orange-red breast and a white abdomen. It is widely distributed through the woodlands of Europe, and in Britain is also a familiar garden bird.

In a more recent work, *Robins and Chats*, the modern-day ornithologist Peter Clement neatly sums up our overall image of this familiar bird:

> A small- to medium-sized, fairly plump chat, with round head, slender tail, red throat and breast, and distinctive melodious song, given year-round. Common or locally common, and widely known as a familiar garden or suburban bird... often celebrated as a symbol of winter on Christmas cards.

A typical robin is about 14 cm (5½ inches) long, with a wingspan of 21 cm (8¼ inches). Like all flying birds, which have evolved special adaptations so they can get airborne, it is much lighter than you might expect: on average an adult robin weighs just 18 grams (less than two thirds of an ounce), a shade over the weight of a couple of new pound coins.

Both male and female robins have that same characteristic and familiar silhouette: plump and perky, with a short tail and upright stance. The two sexes are, to all intents and purposes, identical in appearance: mid-brown above, and white on the lower belly, with a narrow blue-grey band running from the forehead, above the eye, to the sides of the neck. But the most obvious feature of all adult robins is, of course, the red breast, which extends up the bird's face to encompass its sharp bill and beady, black eyes.

2   The Willow Wren

4   The Redbreast

Young robins, which usually appear in our gardens from late spring onwards, are similar in size, shape and behaviour to their parents, but lack the distinctive colourful breast. Instead, their plumage is brown, mottled and speckled with lighter markings above and below. They will not acquire the adult plumage – with those famous orange-red underparts – until the autumn.

We like to think of robins as a distinctively British bird, and yet the species is common and widespread throughout virtually the whole of Europe, from Gibraltar in the south to way beyond the Arctic Circle in the north, as well as being found in parts of North Africa, the Middle East and Central Asia.

Elsewhere in its range, however, the robin is predominantly a shy, woodland bird: as the doyen of twentieth-century ornithologists Max Nicholson pointed out, on the continent robins are rarely found in the kind of open, artificial habitats where we are used to seeing them. Indeed, in a reversal of what we would expect, in the rest of Europe their place alongside human beings in towns and gardens is usually filled by birds we would consider rare and elusive: the redstart, black redstart and nightingale.

Their migratory habits may be different, too. Unlike our mostly sedentary birds, robins in northern and eastern Europe do leave their breeding grounds in autumn, heading south and west to milder climes where food is more reliable – including our own shores, as we shall discover in chapter 10.

Like most of our familiar garden birds, the robin is also a member of the largest of all the world's bird orders: the Passeriformes. This includes almost half the world's species, well over 5,000 in all, of which roughly 4,000 are classified as songbirds.

There are almost a hundred different families of songbirds, from tits to thrushes and larks to buntings, which in turn are split into hundreds of genera. Once thought of as a member of the thrush family, the robin has now been reclassified as one of the Old World Flycatchers. This includes the redstarts, nightingales, wheatears and chats, as well as pied and spotted flycatchers.

The robin may be in a very large family (amongst songbirds, only the New World family of tanagers and their allies contains more species), but it is now the only species in its particular genus, *Erithacus*. That's because scientists have recently discovered that the Japanese and Ryukyu robins are not quite so closely related to our own European robin as we once thought.

And yet if you look through any list of the world's birds, you'll find at least a hundred different 'robins', along with many more species with 'robin' as part of their name, such as robin-chats, bush robins and scrub robins. These birds mostly have two things in common: they feed on insects, usually dropping from low perches onto the ground to do so; and many have a noticeable red (or occasionally pink or yellow) breast.

The reason so many unrelated species carry the name 'robin' is simple. When pioneering sailors and explorers from Britain landed in different parts of the world, and came across any small, perky bird with colourful underparts, they were often reminded of their favourite bird back home. So it was only natural that, homesick for friends and family, they gave it the name 'robin'. As David Lack noted, with more than a hint of imperial pride, 'There is hardly a corner of the world in which the English have not managed to find some red-breasted bird which they could call a robin.'

Today, around the world, we can find the Siberian blue robin, the New Zealand robin, the rose robin of Australia, the cloud-forest robin of Indonesia and Papua New Guinea, the Pacific robin of Polynesia, and the American robin. This last species is actually a member of the thrush family, a close cousin of our own blackbird. It was first described in 1766 by the Swedish nomenclaturist Linnaeus, though the name was probably in use long before then. The American robin is, of course, the species that inspired two popular songs: 'When the Red, Red Robin (Comes Bob, Bob, Bobbin' Along)', a hit for Al Jolson in 1926, and 'Rockin' Robin', written in the late 1950s and taken into the pop charts in 1972 by Michael Jackson and the Jackson 5.

At first sight, this lumbering, bulky thrush is nothing like our own familiar robin, being almost twice as long, and more than four times as heavy. But as it turns towards you, those deep rusty-red underparts are vaguely reminiscent of the much smaller bird we know from back home.

I like to think that, soon after the *Mayflower* landed in November 1620 in what would come to be called New England, one of the Pilgrim Fathers noticed this confiding, red-breasted bird, turned to his companion and announced, 'Look – they have robins here too!'

The robin has spread its fame – or at least its name – around the world. It comes as a surprise, then, to discover that for most of its existence alongside us, the robin was not actually called by that name at all. Instead, it was known as either 'ruddock' or 'redbreast'.

Ruddock comes from the same root as 'ruddy', and refers to the bird's reddish plumage. 'The ruddock warbles soft,' wrote the sixteenth-century poet Edmund Spenser in *Epithalamion*, while in the early nineteenth century Thomas Hood described 'the sweet and shrilly ruddock, with its bleeding breast'. Anglo-Saxon in origin, the appellation persisted well into the Victorian era, and indeed is still sometimes used in Scots dialect even today.

Redbreast is a later name, first appearing in the fifteenth century, and being widely used all the way up to the middle of the twentieth. Indeed, as recently as 1952 the British Ornithologists' Union's checklist still showed the species' official name as 'redbreast'.

That's because 'Robin' was not originally a name at all, but a nickname. Just as people of my grandmother's generation used to refer to the 'Jenny Wren', and 'Tom Tit', so this familiar species was given the alliterative nickname 'Robin Redbreast'.

The Christian name Robin (along with the female equivalent Robyn) is a diminutive of Robert, both names coming across the Channel with the Norman invaders in 1066. But the use of 'robin' as a bird's name is confined to Britain, and so must have arisen here rather than in France, sometime after the Norman Conquest. The first written reference to the bird name 'robin' (without the accompanying 'redbreast') appears in an anonymous Scots poem in 1549, but it is likely to have been in use far earlier than this.

The solving of one puzzle, however, only leads to another. Why was the robin, whose breast is not actually red, but more of an orange shade, named the 'redbreast' in the first place? The answer is simple. Although the fruit known as the orange started to appear in Britain during the Middle Ages, the word 'orange' was not used to describe the intermediate colour between red and yellow until 1557, well over a hundred years after the name 'redbreast' was first recorded.

For our anonymous ancestor who coined the name redbreast – probably long before this first written example – the concept of the colour 'orange' simply did not exist. So from that day to this, we have always thought of the robin's breast as red, even though it is actually an orange shade.

*   *   *   *   *   *

By the end of January, in the garden things have taken a turn for the worse. After a brief respite of milder weather mid-month, a high-pressure system is hovering over the southern half of the country, in what the weather forecasters call a blocking anticyclone. Normally, clear and cloudless skies would bring low temperatures and severe overnight frosts, but the ground would be clear of snow.

But not this year. Just before the anticyclone headed south, a warm front arrived from across the Atlantic Ocean, bringing grey clouds laden with moisture. As it passed over southern Britain, the warm air rose above a layer of cold air already there, and that moisture fell as a thick blanket of snow. For our wildlife, this has brought the worst of both worlds: freezing temperatures, plus a layer of white that covers up their much-needed sources of food.

Back in the garden, the robin is now in a struggle to survive. And he's not the only one. There are millions of robins living in Britain's woods and forests, or along farmland hedgerows. They too have discovered that food is scarce, with insects and invertebrates hiding away in nooks and crannies where the birds can't find them, or buried deep beneath a thick layer of snow. In desperation, these robins have left their usual homes and headed into villages, towns and suburbs, where they may still find something to eat.

Fortunately for both the resident garden robins and these new arrivals, the British are famous for their love of birds, and for their generosity when it comes to feeding them – a custom that began almost 1,500 years ago.

The first known example is of a holy man based in Fife, later canonised as St Serf, who sometime in the sixth century tamed a robin by giving it food. But his actions had dramatic consequences: his classmates, envious of his ability to persuade the bird to feed from his hand, sought the bird out and killed it. Then, so the story goes, his friend Kentigern (who was also later canonised, as St Mungo) miraculously brought the little robin back to life.

From those early beginnings, feeding birds fell into abeyance for many hundreds of years. Then the Victorians – known for their charity towards all God's creatures – began to revive the practice. During the harsh and bitter winter of 1890–91, the Victorian nature writer W.H. Hudson observed working men gathering along the side of the River Thames at lunchtime to give scraps of food to the starving birds. This eventually led to the custom of regularly feeding birds in our gardens, so that today, according to the RSPB, more than half of all Britons – at least 14 million households – put out food for their garden birds.

When I was growing up, we used to simply throw out a few kitchen scraps and stale bread onto the back lawn; but today slick, high-tech bird feeders deliver a wide range of specially designed foods such as sunflower hearts, rich in the energy a bird needs to survive the winter cold. As a result, many garden birds – including the robin – are now enjoying population booms.

In this garden, the robin is lucky. The owners regularly provide many different kinds of food: in tubular feeders, on the bird table and, most importantly for robins, on a wooden tray positioned underneath, on the ground.

So on the last day of the month, even before the sun is up, the male robin is awake and alert. As the darkness slowly melts away, he hops down cautiously onto the ground, his breast lit up by the thin light reflecting up from the snow. He moves forward, each tiny hop leaving behind a pair of prints etched into the crystalline white: three tiny toes in front and one behind.

He must be careful, for along with the hour before dusk this is the most dangerous time of day. All sorts of dangers may be lurking in the dense, dark shrubbery. Even at this early hour, the local sparrowhawk will be keeping his piercing yellow eyes open for likely targets.

Today, though, all seems safe. The robin hops the couple of inches up onto the wooden platform, where a cock blackbird is already feeding greedily. He adopts a submissive pose, keeping his head turned away from the larger bird; but the blackbird is so hungry he does not care who shares his space. So the robin begins to feed, picking up each energy-rich sunflower heart or grain of corn, and swallowing it whole – like other birds, robins don't have teeth, and so do not chew their food.

Several minutes later, he at last begins to slow down. He knows he can rely on this handy service station for the rest of the day, and hopefully throughout this cold spell. But just as the robin is about to retreat into the safety of the nearby bushes, he becomes aware of another bird: one whose presence may prove to be either a threat or an opportunity.

For a moment, he assumes the worst: that this is a rival male, either from the next-door garden or perhaps farther afield. If it is, then there can be no room for sentimentality. Any other male is not just a rival for food – that would be fine, given that he is already sharing this bounty with a host of other species – but more crucially a contender for his territory.

If a male intruder can overthrow this robin, then his future is threatened. If he cannot in turn find another territory, and eject the incumbent male, his chances of breeding are close to zero. But if this stranger turns out to be a female robin, then the cloud that brought the snow will have provided a silver lining, in the form of a potential mate.

The robin does what he always does when confronted with a newcomer in his space. He drops down to the ground, spreads his wings to make himself appear larger, and puffs out his throat and chest so that the colour glows even more brightly. The overall effect is undoubtedly impressive; but will it provoke an attack, or something altogether more desirable?

The other robin pauses and tilts its head on one side as if checking out the scenario for itself. It leans forward and picks up another seed: a prelude to violence, or a way of showing submissiveness? Then it hops a short distance to the left, and continues to feed.

This shows the male robin that the new arrival is a female, posing not a threat, but an opportunity. Although she looks thinner than she should, her plumage is still neat and glossy. Given the cold weather of the past few days, this female robin appears to be in pretty good shape. He acknowledges her presence by flitting up onto a low branch and uttering a few short phrases, to which she responds by cocking her head once again. Then he hops back down and feeds alongside her, hardly noticing a soft rustle in the nearby bushes. Alarm over – all is well.

But in his fascination with this new arrival, he has forgotten something. For any small bird, alertness is the key. And he has momentarily dropped his guard.

He hears another rustle in the bushes; a signal to which, had he not been distracted by the female, he would already have responded. A fraction of a second later, he notices a brief but distinct movement out of the corner of his eye.

Now alarm bells begin to ring. He drops the seed he was about to eat, and stands up straight. As he does so, his fears are confirmed: the cock blackbird, which until that moment had been feeding on the snow-covered lawn, flies rapidly away. As it does so, it issues a rapid series of harsh, discordant calls like the sound of a machine-gun going off: the classic alarm to warn of a predator close by.

Time seems to go into slow motion. The male robin flexes the muscles that power his wings, lowers himself down on spring-loaded legs, and takes flight. At that very moment the neighbour's cat launches itself through the air like a trapeze artist, and snatches its tiny, helpless victim with its front paws. Sharp claws close on the feathers, and then bite into the tender flesh below, drawing tiny red spots of blood. As her heart stops, the female robin issues a brief, soft breath, like the snuffing of a candle.

The male robin has, miraculously, escaped. As the cat leapt forward, his reactions were just enough to allow him to fly clear, though he could feel the rush of air from the animal's movement as it swept beneath him.

But the little female was not so lucky. Exhausted from the rigours of simply finding enough food to survive, she simply could not react quickly enough. She will end up as a grisly and unwelcome offering on the doormat. In the meantime, for the male robin, things are back to where they were: he may have a territory, but he is still searching for a mate.

There is a little bird rather celebrated for its affection to mankind than its singing, which, however, in our climate has the sweetest note of all others... The note of other birds is louder, and their inflexions more capricious, but this bird's voice is soft, tender and well supported, and the more to be valued as we enjoy it the greatest part of the winter.

Oliver Goldsmith, from *A History of the Earth: and Animated Nature*, 1774

FEBRUARY

A chill February wind blows through the reeds, producing a gentle but persistent hum. My boot-clad feet crunch through the early morning frost as a flock of starlings, fugitives from their night-time roost, fly across the horizon – heading off towards their feeding grounds, somewhere out on the coast. The newly risen sun illuminates the pale trunks of the silver birches, and the bitter cold penetrates my gloves so that my fingers are beginning to feel numb.

Here on the Somerset Levels, all is quiet as I walk along the wooded drove, the ancient path down which, centuries ago, sheep and cattle were taken to market across this waterlogged landscape. Not a single bird is singing: the freezing weather has seen to that. Many have fled further south and west to escape the cold snap; those that remain are too busy finding food to think about anything else.

I notice a brief but definite movement in a flattened clump of bracken that forms the border between the path and the reed bed; then another, followed by a loud, metallic 'tic'. Then the bird itself pops up like a sentinel, and confirms its identity: a robin.

I'm visiting my local patch, a hidden fragment of the much larger Avalon Marshes, a newly formed wetland in the heart of the West Country. Here, bitterns boom, great white egrets flap lazily across the reeds, and otters roam, only occasionally revealing their presence when a sleek, glossy-brown animal lollops across the path in front of me, then vanishes as rapidly as it first appeared.

As I take my regular walk around the same circuit, once or twice a week throughout the year, I almost always come across robins. I sometimes wonder what they are doing here, far from either the sanctuary of gardens or their ancestral woodland home. What can they possibly find to sustain themselves in this vast reed bed, a vertical world of stiff, tall grasses, whose roots are encased in murky water and mud?

Yet they must be finding food, for they are always here, their comforting, reliable presence underpinning the seasonal shifts, during which other species come and go on their global journeys. In winter the adjacent lake is home to a phalanx of whistling wigeon, all the way from Iceland or even Siberia. In spring and summer, swallows and house martins flit overhead, seizing invisible insects from the clear blue sky, before they depart again for Africa. And in late July, a clear, pure whistle from the peat diggings signals the presence of a green sandpiper, a passage migrant to our shores, stopping off to feed on its long journey south.

But like the goldcrests following the flocks of blue and great tits in the trees, the wrens and dunnocks skulking around the scrubby foliage along the droves, and the roe deer that leap out in front of me from time to time, scaring me half to death, this robin is a permanent resident. Global wanderings are not to its taste – it prefers to stay put, gambling on its ability to find food in the same place all year round. So to me this robin is like an old friend – someone I expect to see, and miss on the rare occasions when I do not – one of the few constants in a world of almost perpetual change.

In this man-made habitat, created from disused peat diggings, this bird and its cousins can find what they need to survive: plenty of small insects and other invertebrates in spring and summer, and seeds and berries during the autumn and winter. There may not be bird tables or seed feeders – our garden birds' equivalent of the local convenience store – but on the plus side there are fewer competitors, allowing these wetland robins to find just enough food to survive through until next spring.

At least, that is true in normal winters. But with the onset of global climate change, is any winter 'normal' anymore? Each year seems to surprise us more than the last – either because it is far milder than we expect, or far colder. I am (just) too young to remember the Big Freeze of 1962-63, but I do recall shiver-

ROBIN RED-BREAST.

ing as I walked to school in the late 1960s and 1970s. Later on, after a long run of mild winters in the 1990s and the first decade of the new millennium, in 2009-10 and 2010-11 we endured two of the coldest winters on record.

Since then the thermostat seems to have flipped back the other way: during a visit to the Avalon Marshes on a fine, sunny day in December 2015 I heard seven different species of songbird. As well as the usual robins and wrens there were chiffchaffs, which, although they now overwinter here in the south-west, rarely – if ever – sing until March. So how does this topsy-turvy weather affect our favourite bird, the robin?

Eight decades ago, when David Lack was carrying out the first intensive studies of robins at Dartington in South Devon, winters were on average far colder than they are today – even in the traditionally milder south-west of England. Even so, the impulse to breed drove the robins there to pair up and begin to hold territories far earlier than he had originally suspected:

> Tradition assigns St Valentine's Day for the pairing-up of wild birds, which, since most British birds do not nest until at least the end of March, I used to suppose was much too early. But observations at Dartington showed that, far from this being too early, the first robin pairs were formed in the middle of December, over three months before the birds nest, while by 14 February almost all the pairs had been formed.

Birds do not all behave in the same way when it comes to forming pairs. Some, like the mute swan, famously pair for life, the bond only being broken when one partner dies and the other is forced to seek a new mate. Migrants such as the swallow pursue the opposite strategy: the male arrives back in late March or early April, to try to grab the best territory before his rivals. He then waits for a few days until the females return, and only then do they pair up, with nesting following almost immediately. The robin's relative the nightingale, which like the swallow is a long-distance migrant from Africa, follows the same plan, which explains why in the last week of April or the first week of May you may hear nightingales singing in broad daylight – they are so desperate to persuade a female to join them that they perform at every opportunity, by day as well as night.

Resident species such as the robin take a middle course. They rarely live long enough to get more than one or two attempts at breeding, so it makes sense to find a mate as early as they can – sometimes even before Christmas, and almost always by the middle of February.

Until well into the last century, it was widely assumed that male birds – and indeed all other creatures – took the lead in choosing a mate. The idea that dominant males were in charge over the submissive females suited the ornithologists of that time, who were almost all men.

But during the course of the twentieth century, this mistaken theory was gradually overturned. Simple observation showed that although the male usually takes the lead in visual displays (in colourful birds such as the peacock), and also in singing to defend a territory (in songbirds such as the robin), it is the female who makes the final choice.

This even applies in birds such as the black grouse and capercaillie, which pursue a strategy during which the strikingly plumaged males perform in groups (known as 'leks') to show off to their potential mates; and also in mammals that have an annual rut, such as red and fallow deer. It may be the males making all the fuss, noise and bother; but it's the female who holds the cards, as she will make the final choice.

One reason for this is that male robins stay put on their territories, as they have to not only win a mate but also stop rival males from muscling in.

Meanwhile, because they have no territory to defend, the females have the freedom to wander around a local area checking out a succession of males. They do so first thing in the morning, soon after the break of dawn, the time when the males' song is at its loudest and most intense.

What is the female looking for when she enters the male's realm for the first time? The easy, obvious answer is that she is judging the 'quality' of the male – rating either his song, his appearance or both, in an avian version of *The X-Factor* or *The Voice*. We may speculate on whether a male with a louder song, more aggressive behaviour or a larger territory would win a mate more easily and quickly, but this is impossible to answer, as we cannot see into the mind of any bird. It is likely that several factors play their part: for example, one territory might be smaller than another, but provide more food, so might be preferred by the female over the larger one.

The actual process of pair-formation is quite complex, with the hen flying up to the cock and then retreating, and a lot of exaggerated posturing by both birds, followed by quieter spells when one or both will retreat and pick up food, or engage in a spot of preening.

The pioneer of animal behaviour studies, Sir Julian Huxley, first noted this odd tendency of courting birds to partake in other, seemingly unrelated, activities when he studied great crested grebes before the First World War; but it took another great scientist, Niko Tinbergen, to coin a name for it: 'displacement activity'. The theory is that this is a way of reducing tension, and also allows each bird to size up their next move: do they want to continue with their relationship, and make their liaison more permanent, or stop and try with another potential suitor?

Male robins may also be quite fierce towards their potential mate. This may at first seem rather odd – but try seeing the situation from the incumbent male's point of view. Until now he has defended his territory against all-comers for the whole of the winter; yet now he has to lower his guard and welcome this virtual stranger into his home. He may not even recognise her immediately – as we have seen, male and female robins are identical in plumage and appearance – and although she knows he is a male (because he is singing), he cannot at first be sure about her. No wonder he may have mixed feelings about this newcomer on his home patch.

After that initial phase of suspicion and enquiry, the process of forming a pair goes on for another two or three days, though at a less intense level. The male follows the female around his territory, singing much more quietly than before, as if trying to show her that his initial aggression was misplaced, and that he now wants her to stay.

By the end of this second phase they are a breeding pair, and what has been called their 'engagement period' begins, during which the male returns to full song. The two generally stay apart from one another during this time, though we know that the male can recognise his mate, as he ignores her while still chasing out any other intruders.

In some winters, even after the male and female robin have paired up, there is a cold snap, with snow and ice making the finding of food – indeed, surviving at all – much more difficult. Sometimes the pair will split up – usually only temporarily – and search for food elsewhere. On very rare occasions the male and female will even split their territory down the middle and begin to act aggressively towards one another. But unless the cold spell is particularly long and harsh, they will usually stick it out together.

Even after they have paired up, robins do not stay particularly close to one another. That's because each bird is more interested in finding food than in courtship and breeding, which is still several weeks, maybe even more than a month, away.

ROBIN. Courtship Display.

I decide to test out the hypothesis that the behaviour of robins in our towns and cities might differ from that of their country cousins. Back in my home city of London, spring comes several weeks earlier than elsewhere in Britain. Partly, of course, that's because London is situated in the warmer south-east of England. But there is another reason: the 'urban heat-island effect'.

This is a phenomenon created by the ability of buildings to retain warmth, together with the heat released by millions of vehicles – and it means that in late winter, nights are often four or five degrees warmer than in the surrounding areas. And that means that London's robins should be able to get a crucial head start over their rural relatives.

In the very heart of the capital, just north of King's Cross Station and alongside the Regent's Park Canal, lies a hidden haven for wildlife.

Camley Street Natural Park was created back in the idealistic days of the mid-1980s, and despite being on land that, were it to be developed, would be worth a vast sum, it has somehow survived. On a sunny but chilly February day, moorhens bicker, celandines and primroses look as if they have been out for weeks. Above the constant sound of traffic, building works and passers-by, a robin is singing amongst the still-bare twigs of an ash tree.

He's not alone. A cock blackbird chinks crossly, while dunnocks warble, wrens trill, coots chip and a goldcrest – so high-pitched I can only just hear him – sings his rhythmic *'twiddly-twiddly-tweeee'* song, somewhere out of sight in the dark depths of a conifer.

But it's the robin's song that cuts through the surrounding noise, lending a bucolic feeling to this quintessentially urban soundscape. I suspect he has not only established his territory and found a mate, as you might expect by now, but may also have begun to nest.

Studies have shown that birds living in cities do breed significantly earlier than their rural counterparts. Partly, as already noted, this is down to the warmer microclimate produced by the urban heat-island effect, which applies in all large cities, whatever their latitude. But although it may seem counter-intuitive to say so, cities also provide more food than the surrounding countryside.

Our habit of feeding garden birds – not just during the winter but nowadays in spring too – means that there is usually a plentiful, reliable supply of energy-rich food within easy reach of any urban robin's territory. We also provide food unwittingly, through our wasteful habits. And insects, too, appear earlier in the year in cities, and are often more abundant: partly because of the warmer temperature, but also because, unlike the countryside, the land has not been sprayed with lethal insecticides.

There's one other reason why urban birds begin breeding earlier than rural ones: light. Due to the artificial lighting in our streets, homes and workplaces, cities are far brighter at night than the countryside. Even a small amount of extra light in spring can advance the development of the hormones that drive the breeding cycle by up to four weeks.

For some species, such as the blue tit, this does not confer much of an advantage, as they only ever have a single brood of chicks, and so may be better off waiting until the full onset of spring. But for the robin, which usually has two, and sometimes three, broods, getting the breeding season off to an early start means that they have a far better chance of raising more chicks – just so long as there isn't an unexpected cold snap later in the spring.

Before this urban robin here in London can begin to think of a second – or even a first – brood, he must go through the second stage of the breeding process: courtship. This is distinct from pair formation, though it does overlap in terms of behaviour.

In many birds, courtship displays are long, ornate and highly complex. The 'penguin dance' of great crested grebes is a good example. After a long and complicated build-up, involving countless examples of displacement activity such as preening, the two birds stand up in the water, paddling furiously to stay upright, and wave waterweed at one another. The display of the male peacock, as he fans his huge feathers out while strutting up and down, is another classic example of a courtship display at its most arresting.

Disappointingly for us, robin courtship is a far briefer and more circumspect affair; indeed, it is often one of those 'blink-and-you-miss-it' moments. Even the colourful breast, so crucial when it comes to seeing off rivals, is hardly relevant – instead, the male and female get down to the business of mating almost immediately, with little or no wooing.

The only exception to this is the phenomenon known as 'courtship feeding', in which the male will sometimes offer food to the female. Again, the female often seems to initiate this process, when she gives a brief, single-note call, and quivers her wings, which prompts the male to approach her with a morsel of food. The early-nineteenth-century poet Robert Bloomfield – a rival to John Clare as a chronicler of rural life – celebrated this intimate behaviour in this characteristically well observed verse:

> E'en as the red-breast, sheltering in a bower,
> Mourns the short darkness of a passing shower,
> Then, while the azure sky extends around,
> Darts on a worm that breaks the moistened ground,
> And mounts the dripping fence with joy elate,
> And shares the prize triumphant with his mate.

Watching this ritual, which also occurs in many other birds, I am reminded of a parent bird feeding a youngster – which indeed is exactly what this looks like. There is something extraordinarily intimate about the whole process, which has evolved to strengthen the bond between the male and female. It is also a crucial prelude to the next and most important step in the process: mating, which, as with many other songbirds, is so brief and perfunctory it is easy to miss it entirely.

As soon as I walk out of the gate, the robin's sweet notes begin to fade, and a minute or two later, I can hear no birdsong at all – not even the chirping of sparrows. How important a semi-natural haven like Camley Street Natural Park seems, as I walk back towards the hustle and bustle of King's Cross Station, to the millions of people who live and work in this noisy, crowded city.

It has long been assumed that birdsong is somehow good for us – that, even though we know its function is purely biological, it still has a beneficial effect on our emotions and feelings, and enhances our sense of well-being. Oddly, it was only very recently that studies finally proved this to be true, by separating the benefits we gain from simply being outdoors in a green setting from the specific effects of birdsong.

The conclusion of these studies was just as we might have expected: that listening to the songs of birds makes us feel calmer and happier; especially if it is a sound we associate with a bird we know and love. And few birds are better known or more loved than the robin.

It is the first mild day of March:
Each minute sweeter than before.
The redbreast sings from the tall larch
That stands beside our door.

There is a blessing in the air,
Which seems a sense of joy to yield
To the bare trees, and mountains bare,
And grass in the green field.

William Wordsworth, 'To My Sister', 1798

MARCH

I'm on the Tarka Trail near Barnstaple in North Devon, a couple of weeks before the Equinox, and on this fine March morning the first signs of spring are undoubtedly here. But today I'm not looking for otters, but something altogether more unusual and intriguing.

Little clumps of primroses – whose name appropriately comes from the Latin, meaning 'first flower' – adorn the side of the path, while a bumblebee, the first I've seen this year, has taken to the air in search of life-giving nectar. There may be a chill in the air, but blue skies and a strengthening sun promise a warm and pleasant day ahead.

The path I'm ambling along was once the railway line between Barnstaple and Torrington. Axed by the infamous Dr Beeching in 1965, half a century later it has been reborn as the ideal spot for a Sunday-morning outing for local people. And here they come: Lycra-clad cyclists sporting every conceivable shade of yellow, blue and pink; a dutiful dad, pushing his toddler in a buggy while an older child balances precariously on his shoulders; and a bevy of dog-walkers being tugged along by their eager pets.

All have come here to enjoy a walk in the countryside. But such casual leisure activities are not for me. For I am on a quest – or, more specifically, a 'twitch': a special journey to see an individual rare bird, which I may or may not succeed in finding. As always on such days, I feel a sense of excited anticipation, for although this particular bird is a robin, it is no ordinary one. It may sound the same, it may even behave in the same manner, but in appearance, it could hardly be more different. Now all I have to do is find it.

The path, and the trees and bushes either side of it, are alive with birds. Chaffinches and blackbirds hop along a few yards in front of me, turning over the leaf litter with their bills to reveal seeds and insects to eat. A great tit yells its *'tea-cher, tea-cher'* song, a riot of jaunty syncopation, while dunnocks warble and wrens trill above the constant hum of the nearby main road.

Robins are here, too: lots of them. There seems to be another new territory, defended by yet another singing male, every few yards along the Trail. One showy bird perches in full view on an early-budding ash tree, and pours out his song. But, handsome though he undoubtedly is, he is not the bird I am looking for. So although I am tempted to stop and enjoy this marvellous close-up view of a robin singing in the spring sunshine, I walk on.

I had never realised before just how skulking male robins can sometimes be. Further along the path I can hear at least three, each in full song, but infuriatingly none are actually in view. I peer through a tangle of hawthorn twigs, but cannot see where they are sitting. It strikes me as ironic that, although I am struggling to find robins, I can pick out far more elusive species, such as a male bullfinch, resplendent in cherry-pink, or a tiny goldcrest, hovering on blurred wings to glean even tinier insects in the ever-warming sun. Nearby, a nuthatch creeps confidently down a tree trunk, showing off its steel-blue and rusty-orange plumage, and the black bandit mask across its eyes.

I reach what I am told is the right spot, where I can hear three more singing robins. Surely one bird in this trio will be the one I have come to see. A grey squirrel scampers ominously along a branch – too early to steal eggs for now, but it will return to do so later in the season.

I see the first robin, and the second – both, once again, typical birds. The third, further along the path, seems to have fallen silent, and so I resort to new technology. I take out my smartphone and find an app that plays the robin's song. But before I can press the 'Play' button, a dad and his daughter stop their bikes and ask me if I am looking for anything in particular. The girl, aged about nine, points excitedly towards the tree, and for a brief moment I think she has found what I am searching for. But it turns out to be a hoverfly, fixed in mid-air on whirring wings. Miraculous, but not what I am here to find.

Father and daughter cycle on, and I press the button on my phone and wait, hardly daring to breathe – for time is rapidly running out. I promised my family I would be back for Sunday lunch, and so this is surely my last hope. The robin's familiar sound fills the morning air, and almost immediately a small bird flies directly over my head and lands in the tree nearby. I lift my binoculars and there, finally, is the bird I have been searching for. A robin – but one with a difference.

The robin I've come here to see is not a 'redbreast' at all, but a ghostly apparition in grey and white, lacking any of the familiar chocolate-brown and orange-red shades of his commoner cousins. Otherwise, he is clearly a robin: the cocked tail, black, beady eye and jerky, flitting movements are quite simply unmistakable.

THE ROBIN: A BIOGRAPHY

On a closer look I can see that this bird is a delicate shade of dove-grey on the crown, nape, back, tail and wings, with a slight but definite brownish tinge to the edges of its flight feathers. The forehead, face and breast are a soft creamy-white, merging into a marginally paler shade of grey on the belly and flanks. The legs are grey-brown, the bill grey and the eye – as with every robin – jet-black. I wonder what the first person to stumble across this bird must have thought when they saw it. I would have assumed it was an ultra-rare Asian chat or flycatcher, brought here on easterly winds. However, as soon as the bird begins to move – and open his bill to sing – his true identity immediately becomes clear.

He is not showing himself easily, almost as if, being so different, he is wary of drawing attention to his presence. His territory, too, backing onto the Royal Marines' barracks – old Nissen huts and pieces of litter blown against a wire fence – is less aesthetically pleasing than the others: an unsuitable backdrop for such an unusual and striking bird.

But gradually, he becomes less shy, and begins to emerge fully into view, perching on a prickly strand of rose above the mass of brambles. Then he flies a short distance to perch on a twig next to a tree trunk.

For me, this is an extraordinary moment. I have been familiar with robins since I was a young child – for more than fifty years. Indeed, I cannot really remember *not* knowing what a robin looked like. During my lifetime, I must have seen thousands – perhaps tens of thousands – of robins: in woods and gardens, along the coast and in reed beds, and every single one (apart, of course, from the speckled juveniles) has looked exactly the same as any other.

But not this bird. And now he sits and sings for me, balancing effortlessly on a branch hanging over the path, bobbing his head and flicking his tail between phrases, and occasionally pausing to preen his wing feathers before resuming his song.

I play the birdsong app on my phone for a second time, and he responds exactly how I would have predicted: flitting closer to me and, looking down from his dominant perch above my head, singing even louder and longer than before.

Meanwhile a sparrowhawk soars high in the sky overhead. A flock of gold-finches tinkle, and two wrens perform a duet either side of me in an avian face-off. Spring really does feel just around the corner.

Over the next three months, robins enter the race to reproduce, the most critical period in their short and busy lives. I take my leave of the Tarka Trail, hoping that this very special pastel-shaded robin does manage to survive, attract a mate and raise a family of his own.

So why is this ghostly bird so different from millions of other of singing male robins in Britain?

He is not, clearly, an albino – the dark (rather than pink) eye and uniformly grey upperparts rule that out. Nor is he, as some observers have suggested, leucistic – missing all the normal pigments. When I get back home, to find out exactly why this bird is such an unusual colour, I contact an expert on unusual bird plumages: Hein van Grouw, Senior Curator of Birds at the Natural History Museum.

Hein explains that both the pigments in the robin's normal plumage – eumelanin and phaeomelanin – have become diluted. The eumelanin, the same pigment found in brown and black hair and skin, may be slightly less diluted than the reddish or yellowish-brown phaeomelanin, but both are still present in small amounts, which explains why the breast and crown are not pure white, but have a creamy tint. Hein calls this dual lack of pigment 'Dilution Pastel'.

This trait is not unique to this particular bird: over the past decade similar individuals have been seen in Yorkshire and Kent, and coincidentally a second grey and white bird has also been found just down the road, a little further along the Tarka Trail. But since there are at least six million breeding pairs of robins in Britain, it is still very rare. Given the familiarity and tameness of robins, we can also be sure that these unusual-looking birds are likely to be reported if they turn up elsewhere – whether at a migration hotspot or on a bird table in a suburban garden.

You might think that their odd appearance would affect these birds' breeding success. Yet there is clear evidence that they are able to pair up with normal-coloured females, which suggests that, despite the widely held belief that the orange-red breast is crucial for defending a robin's territory, and for attracting a mate, it may not be quite so important after all.

Back in the garden, soon after dawn one day in the middle of March, a male robin perches on the topmost twig of an apple tree, showing off his breast in the weak, early-morning sunlight. But before he can even open his beak to deliver his first burst of song, he is distracted by a brief movement in the foliage of the adjacent tree, accompanied by a sharp, urgent, ticking sound. He cocks his head to listen more closely, and hears it again, louder this time.

Then the maker of that sound emerges: another robin. She is a female, whose own mate holds the territory in the garden next door. But, having just paired up, she is still unsure where her mate's territory ends and that of his rival begins.

She doesn't remain in any doubt for long: the incumbent male, sensing a threat to his little kingdom, has swooped down to chase her away. He fluffs out his breast feathers and postures in front of her before taking to the wing and chasing her back where she came from. If she was unsure of the boundaries of the two territories before, she can surely have no doubts now.

Yet that's not the end of the matter. For her own mate has seen what has been going on, and has arrived to support his partner. This, in turn, has alerted the defending robin's mate, so now there are four birds involved in the row.

The two males take the lead: wings out and claws forward, they launch themselves into the air in a flurry of feathers, while their mates urge them on with equally hostile retaliatory gestures. After a few minutes have passed, however, the intruding male decides that discretion may be the better part of valour, and beats a hasty retreat. Residents 1, Incomers 0.

As the breeding season goes on, and both pairs establish the position of their territories more clearly, these border skirmishes will become less and less frequent. When they do occur, they are usually settled by both males singing loudly across the territorial border, like quarrelling neighbours shouting at one another across the garden fence.

By the end of May or June, when both pairs are busy feeding their demanding broods of young, their early rivalry will have dwindled so much that all four birds may be seen hopping across the same patch of grass in search of worms, with no sign of antagonism. Yet in August they will be at it again, in preparation for establishing their territories for the coming autumn and winter.

During his early career as a schoolmaster in Devon in the years leading up to the Second World War, David Lack studied robins more closely than anyone had ever done before – and few have matched since. He discovered that, although rival males do occasionally fight to the death, such events are rare. After all, if the conflict gets too violent, then both birds know they are at risk of dying or being seriously injured, and will usually retreat.

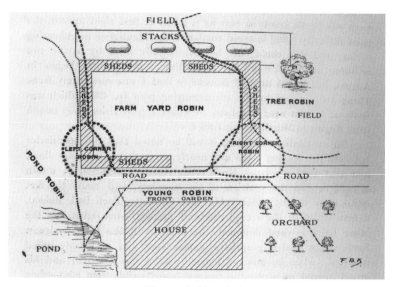

FIELD

STACKS

SHEDS · SHEDS

FARM YARD ROBIN

TREE ROBIN

FIELD

LEFT CORNER ROBIN

RIGHT CORNER ROBIN

SHEDS

ROAD · ROAD

YOUNG ROBIN
FRONT GARDEN

ORCHARD

HOUSE

POND

POND ROBIN

F.B.A

Diagram of robin territories

So instead, they resort to gestures: ritual signals of aggression that state their intentions clearly, without actually leading to physical contact – indeed, many of these gestures are expressly designed to minimise the need to fight. Just like the behaviour shown by the male and female when they first started to pair up in February, this is a kind of displacement activity, though this time between two males.

Lack observed such behaviour many times in robins, concluding that it helped defuse tension at moments of high drama. Interestingly, he went a step further, comparing it with aspects of our own behaviour, and pointing out that 'the same is seen when two small boys prepare to engage in doubtful combat'.

He might have just as easily compared the rival male robins to two young men facing each other off in a nightclub, using clear gestures to stake their claim over their own space (and, often, a woman), yet also managing subconsciously to signal that the last thing they actually want to do is fight.

March is the time when the breeding season really gets going – not just for the robin, but for all our resident birds. The passing of the Equinox in the third week of the month marks the shift between winter and spring, when for the first time in six months there is more available light than darkness.

More light means more time available to find food, and as the growing season for plants begins to get underway, so too the first insects begin to emerge. On fine, sunny days towards the end of the month there may be four different species of butterfly on the wing. Canary-yellow brimstones vie for our attention with gaudy, false-eyed peacocks, variegated small tortoiseshells and the handsome black and orange commas, whose underwing reveals the curious curved white marking that looks just like a punctuation mark, and gives this distinctive butterfly its name.

For the robin, early spring also sees the emergence of the smaller insects such as beetles and ants, which make up the main body of its diet. But robins have not become as common and widespread as they are by being fussy eaters: they will take a wide range of insect food, including moths and small butterflies, bees and slugs, wasps and woodlice, earthworms and earwigs. At other times of year, when the opportunity arises or insect food is scarce, they will feed on fruit and seeds, including whatever we choose to put out on our bird tables.

For now, though, more light, more warmth and more insects trigger something in the brains of our resident songbirds, including the robin. The process of courtship is at an end, and the hard work of building a nest and raising a family is about to begin.

The timing of the breeding cycle in most birds is very much a movable feast, and robins are no exception. Nest-building usually takes place towards the end of March, but they do sometimes make nests much earlier, in January and February, and even occasionally before the turn of the year, in November and December.

Such early nesting is far more frequent than it used to be, especially during very mild winters, but these unseasonable breeding attempts usually end in failure. However, there are instances where robins have successfully raised young to the point of fledging in the middle of winter.

But in a typical year, that increase in daylight marked by the Spring Equinox on or around 21 March is the trigger for nest-building to begin. The female starts to gather material, usually close to where she intends the nest to be made. Robins' nests are built on a foundation of dead leaves, gathered from where they fell last autumn. The next layer consists of soft moss, on top of which the bird places a layer of hair, grass or feathers to form a shallow cup in which she will lay her clutch of eggs.

Considering that the robin is such a common and familiar bird, its nest can be surprisingly hard to find. This is partly because when building the female takes care not to draw attention to herself: she takes her time, bringing material back to the site only infrequently, so that the whole nest may take three or four days to complete. The male gets away without having to do all the hard work, a situation very different from that of the wren, whose males must construct several 'cock's nests', each carefully inspected by the female until she finds the one she considers most suitable.

Of all Britain's birds, robins choose to nest in a greater variety of unusual places than any other species. Today's birders – however expert they may be – are often unaware of this, simply because over the past few decades, since egg collecting was rightly made illegal, the practice of nest finding has declined too.

But our Victorian ancestors were dab hands at tracking down the location of birds' nests. One such expert was a man of the cloth, the Reverend John Christopher Atkinson. Born in 1814, a year before the Battle of Waterloo, Atkinson lived a long and fruitful life, surviving (just) into the twentieth century. As a boy, he lived in rural Essex, where, like his contemporaries, he learned to find nests and collect eggs.

Later he turned this boyhood knowledge to good use, in 1861 publishing a slim volume, *British Birds' Eggs and Nests, Popularly Described*, in which he readily acknowledged that much of his practical knowledge had been gained on those early egg-collecting expeditions. The book was very popular, running to at least sixteen editions, and was still being widely read long after the author's death, inspiring many generations of egg collectors and, it is to be hoped, ornithologists.

In his entry on the robin, Atkinson writes with undisguised enthusiasm about the species' predilection for choosing unusual nest-sites, which presumably added to the challenge of finding its nest and eggs:

> A hundred different places, too, the little bird selects for the site of its nest...
>
> In the tilt of a wagon; in a steam-boat; in a room of the cottage; near a blacksmith's forge; in the constantly-used garden shed, as well as in the ivy or evergreen bush; or on the bank, or in the hedge; or in a hole in the old ruin or bank or house-wall; all places seem to suit it alike.

David Lack, too, was well aware of the range of different places used, listing 'a jam-jar, a letter-box, an old boot, a pulpit, a human skull, or even a dead cat'. He also reported that a householder in Birmingham was astonished to discover a pair of robins nesting in his unmade bed, and even chose to make alternative sleeping arrangements until the chicks successfully fledged several weeks later. A pair in Basingstoke bettered even this in terms of speed: 'A gardener hung up his coat in the tool-shed at 9.15 a.m., and when he took it down to go off for lunch at 1 p.m. there was an almost complete nest in one of the pockets.'

Robins have occasionally bred in churches, seeking sanctuary from predators, though sometimes causing theological and practical problems. In at least two cases, dating back to the nineteenth century, they chose to build their nest on an open bible, as it lay on a reading desk. It is not known whether the church authorities chose to let the bird's inconvenient nest-site remain unmolested.

But perhaps the most bizarre instance of all came when a pair of robins in rural Surrey built their nest in a wagon, which was then driven all the way to Worthing in Sussex and back – a return trip of at least 100 miles. One parent was observed to accompany it for the whole journey, assiduously feeding the young as it went.

A later collector of curious aspects of bird behaviour, Mark Cocker, reported in *Birds Britannica* that robins have built their nests in a hole made by a cannonball in the mast of the *Victory* (against which Nelson had been leaning when he was fatally shot), in the engine of a Second World War aircraft (which flew regular sorties complete with nest and eggs) and, as Lack also noted, in the skull of a convict who had been hanged for highway robbery in 1796. As Lack pointed out, from the robin's point of view there is nothing unusual about what we consider to be odd choices of nest-site: 'A robin places its nest in a crevice or hole, and those provided by human beings are as good as, but no better than, natural holes.'

I've never seen a robin's nest in quite such an unusual or grisly setting; but I have seen them in a few peculiar places, such as on a shelf in the garage of our suburban semi-detached home when I was a child. Why this particular pair didn't choose one of the many suitable nest-sites in the garden was hard for me to understand; I probably assumed that they would be safer from predators – and bad weather – indoors. And they almost certainly were.

Once the female robin has finished making her nest, she starts to lay her eggs. An hour or so after the break of dawn she squats down into the neat cup and deposits a single, tiny egg into the centre, where it nestles on the soft lining. Each day that passes, at roughly the same time, she lays another, and another, until her clutch is complete – usually between four and six eggs in all.

The eggs are cream-coloured, with fine markings: reddish-brown blotches, streaks and freckles, providing a limited amount of camouflage against curious intruders. But as with all birds that produce reasonably striking and conspicuous eggs, the female robin sits really tight – also hiding her colourful breast so as not to draw attention to her presence.

We should not underestimate the effort it takes for the female to produce a full clutch of eggs. Each egg is about 2 cm (¾ inch) long and weighs 2.5 grams (just over $\frac{1}{12}$ of an ounce, or about the same as half a sheet of A4 paper), but together that means a full clutch may weigh between 10 and 15 grams ($\frac{1}{3}$ to ½ an ounce). That's between half and three-quarters of her total body weight, at a time, in early spring, when food may be scarce. Imagine a female human being giving birth to quadruplets or quintuplets each weighing 8–10 kg (17–22 lbs) each, and totalling more than 6 stones, and we can begin to appreciate the effort it takes.

Like other songbirds, the hen will not begin to sit until she has laid all her eggs, so the chicks will all hatch at more or less the same time. Only when the clutch is complete does she finally sit tight, and the incubation process begins.

J. W. Frohawk.

FIGS. 1— 4 MISSEL THRUSH.   FIGS. 18—19 RING OUZEL.   FIGS.   24 REDSTART
    5— 9 SONG THRUSH.   20 WHEATEAR.   25—28 REDBREAST.
   10 17 BLACKBIRD.   21—22 WHINCHAT.   29—31 NIGHTINGALE.
                                     23 STONECHAT.

The nest is hid close at its mossy root
Composed of moss and grass and lined with hair
And five brun-coloured eggs snug sheltered there
And bye and bye a happy brood will be
The tennants of this woodland privacy.

John Clare, 'The Robin's Nest', 1835

APRIL

I can still remember the first time I stumbled across a robin's nest. I must have been about eight or nine years old and, as I peered beyond the yellow blooms of a honeysuckle, my eyes gradually became accustomed to the darkness. There, nestling amongst the dark green foliage, was a cup of leaves and grass; resting on a soft layer of green moss were five perfectly formed eggs.

I reached inside and gingerly lifted one out, taking care not to crush the tiny object with my fingers. In the light its colours became visible: a creamy-white background covered with a layer of reddish-brown, as if someone had randomly daubed the surface with rich Devon earth.

I have to confess that for a moment I was tempted to keep this prize for myself. But having taken a blackbird's egg the year before, which I'd kept for weeks in our airing-cupboard until my patience ran out and I opened it up to reveal a tiny and long-dead chick, I no longer had the stomach for egg-collecting. I tried to imagine the baby robin growing inside: that tiny miracle of nature found in every egg, large or small. I knew that taking it would be wrong, and so I replaced it as carefully as I could and, having closed the safety curtain of the honeysuckle leaves and flowers, I left the robins and their nest in peace.

Like many songbirds, the hen robin does all the incubation duties, for about two weeks, day and night, although she does not sit continuously. At this time of year, she loses some of the feathering from her belly, producing a naked area known as a 'brood-patch'. This allows her to transfer the heat from her body to the eggs, enabling the tiny chicks inside to develop and grow.

During this period, she must make sure she keeps her energy levels up, for as soon as the chicks start to hatch she and her mate will have their work cut out to keep them fed. So from time to time she will surreptitiously lift herself up from the nest cup and fly a short distance away to feed, taking care to ensure that there are no predators watching.

If she has not yet left the nest, her mate may utter a brief call – just a few notes – in order to persuade her to come. Sometimes she will then find food for herself, but as often as not the male will feed her, proffering a mouthful of small caterpillars or other insects. But he hardly ever comes to the nest with food – for to do so would be to advertise its presence to the local cats. By providing food he is saving her valuable effort and energy, and minimising the time when she is off the eggs; but also reinforcing the pair bond between the two birds.

This routine continues for roughly two weeks, when the young finally hatch. The female knows this is imminent, for the tiny chick inside the egg will begin to become more active than before. It uses a tiny protuberance on its bill known as an 'egg tooth' to break the hard protective shell, and now the new-born robin can emerge into the bright light of a new and unfamiliar world.

For the male robin, this is when the real work begins. From dawn to dusk each day he flies constantly to and fro, catching tiny insects and caterpillars and bringing them back to feed his hungry, and rapidly growing, brood.

Earlier in the season, when there are fewer hours of daylight, there tend to be smaller broods of four or five chicks. By June, when there is the maximum amount of daylight available for the cock and hen to find food, the second broods usually have six chicks, and occasionally even more – exceptionally, eight young have been raised to the fledging stage.

Not all eggs successfully hatch: on average, almost one-third of all eggs fail to do so, and these are usually left in the nest. However, the parents do remove the opened eggshells soon after the chicks have emerged. Robins, like most songbirds, are very house-proud: they pay a lot of attention to ensuring that the nest is neat and tidy. Young chicks defecate after being fed, but fortunately produce their droppings in faecal sacs – or, as Bill Oddie once memorably described them, 'shrink-wrapped poo' – which allows the parent birds to take them away easily and conveniently, to prevent poor hygiene in the nest. On average, each baby robin can produce a faecal sac every hour or so, keeping the parents pretty busy.

Like all songbirds, robins are born naked, blind and helpless. Yet their urge to survive is incredibly strong: after a few hours they instinctively respond to the male's return, raising themselves up and opening their mouths to reveal a bright yellow gape. This is exactly the response he needs: having dropped off his package of food he immediately flies away to find some more.

About five days after hatching the chicks' eyes begin to open, and they are able to look around their new world for the first time. The first 'pin feathers' start to emerge early on, and by the time the youngsters are eight to eleven days old proper feathers are starting to appear along their back and wings. The tail feathers are the last to grow, just before the chick is ready to leave the nest.

As the chicks get bigger, and begin at last to resemble baby robins rather than miniature dinosaurs, the female is at last able to leave the nest and find food too; indeed, her participation is absolutely essential if the chicks are to reach the point of fledging. Once both parents are bringing back food, the chicks' growth rapidly accelerates. Weighing just 1.7 grams ($\frac{1}{17}$ of an ounce) when they hatch, by the time they fledge their weight has increased more than ten-fold, and they tip the scales at about 18 grams (¾ of an ounce) – roughly the same as their parents.

The chicks usually stay in the nest for two or more weeks, but they may be tempted – or forced by an intruding predator – to leave well before this. But it makes sense to stay in the safety of the nest as long as possible.

When an intruder – even a benevolent one such as a human being – does stray too near, then both parents will do their best to lure them away. Like other birds, they will at first give a series of soft alarm calls, but if the trespasser strays too close then they may try other tactics. This occasionally includes what scientists call a 'distraction display', in which the adult robin hops along the ground holding its wing out as if injured, in a (usually successful) attempt to lure the predator away.

Meanwhile, the chicks will do their best to flatten themselves down inside the nest to make themselves as inconspicuous as possible, which, if they are fully grown, can be rather tricky. They are helped by the speckled pattern of their plumage, which breaks up their outline, so that to a casual observer peering through the foliage they look like leaves illuminated by scattered rays of sunlight.

Occasionally one of the adults is killed away from the nest, either by a predator, by crashing headlong into a glass window, or by being hit by a car. Normally this means the slow death by starvation of the baby robins, as the surviving parent cannot find enough food to meet their needs. But if they are only a few days off fledging, the weather is good and there are plenty of insects for the surviving partner to catch, they may still manage to survive.

Not every chick will make it to the fledging stage. One in five will die before they get that far, either because they have not managed to obtain enough food (when there is a shortage or because their strongest siblings have taken the lion's share) or if the nest is predated, in which case the whole brood will usually perish. Overall, the odds that any one egg will produce a fledged chick are only just better than even, with the greatest success in the middle of the breeding season, rather than at the beginning or the end.

The actual departure from the nest can be a dramatic affair. Remember, these baby birds have never known what life is like outside the comforting cocoon of their home; yet instinctively they are drawn to leaving, especially, perhaps, because by now the cup is so crowded the four surviving chicks can barely fit inside.

For the two or three days before they actually leave, each youngster has practised flapping its perfunctory wings, sometimes, during a particularly vigorous bout of exercise, running the risk that it will topple out altogether. That danger aside, this enables them to strengthen their new flight muscles; they also preen their new wing and tail feathers with their bill to keep them neat and in the best possible condition.

Finally, early one morning, it's time to depart. The male and female usually perch a few metres away, encouraging their offspring by making brief but persistent calls. The largest chick takes the plunge first, frantically flapping its wings and just managing to fly the short distance to a convenient twig, where it perches nervously like a novice on a tightrope.

Soon afterwards, the others follow; and though the last chick often has to be coaxed by its parents, an hour or so after the process began all four chicks are safely out of the nest and begging to be fed by the male. Delay can of course be fatal, as the noise made by the chicks can easily attract unwanted visitors such as the local cat.

Even when the chicks have successfully left the nest, the adults' duties are far from over. Young robins constantly beg for food for about three weeks after fledging, after which time they are finally independent. However, even then they will usually stay close to where they were born, preferring the familiarity of their home to the unknown.

The period when the chicks are being fed away from the nest is the most dangerous for both the youngsters and their parents: when still inside the nest they are as safe as they can be, especially if it is tucked away in dense vegetation. But once they leave its sanctuary, they become immensely vulnerable, and many fall victim to predators. As with all garden birds, domestic cats are the biggest danger, closely followed by sparrowhawks.

Not all robins' breeding attempts go quite to plan. Very rarely – even more rarely now that the species has declined in numbers across much of Britain – a cuckoo will choose a pair of robins as its host.

Early one morning, the female cuckoo will then lay a single egg in the robin's nest, removing any eggs that have already been laid there. Once the cuckoo chick hatches, it is driven by brute instinct to eject any remaining eggs or chicks; while the robin is also driven by another innate impulse to feed this huge and rapidly growing chick – even when it becomes far too big for the nest, and indeed far larger than either of its foster-parents.

Analysis of almost 13,000 nest record cards, submitted by amateur birders to the British Trust for Ornithology between 1939 and 1982, has shown that fewer than 1 in 200 (roughly sixty in all) contained a cuckoo egg or chick. This compares to between 1 in 32 and 1 in 45 for the cuckoo's most popular hosts in Britain, the meadow pipit, reed warbler and dunnock.

In central Europe and Russia, though, the picture is very different. There, the robin is a frequent host for the cuckoo, and as a result cuckoos have evolved the ability to mimic the colour and pattern of robins' eggs, increasing the chances of their own much larger egg not being detected.

Photo by W. Farren

Robin's Nest in an old hat

Very occasionally, male robins may practise bigamy, with two breeding females at the same time. This can only usually happen if the two females both turn up in the male's territory at more or less the same moment. Even when this does occur, the dominant female usually drives the other away. But from time to time they settle down into a *ménage à trois*.

What generally happens is that one female starts nest-building a few days before the other, and so lays her eggs earlier as well. Once the first hen is safely sitting on her clutch, the male can then pay more attention to the second female. Of course, this runs the very real risk that neither nest will be successful, as he is dividing his duties and potentially spreading himself too thinly. But if there is plenty of food available, his gamble may pay off.

On one occasion, in Sussex, two females nested really close to one another in ivy on a garden wall, laid their eggs at more or less the same time, and both managed to successfully rear their young to fledging. Even more unusually, also in Sussex, two female robins both laid their eggs in the same nest, and then both attempted to incubate them. Sadly, the experiment did not work, and the birds deserted.

Such examples of togetherness are, as we have seen, very rare for robins. However endearing they may appear to us, the truth is rather different. (Those readers who will not hear a word spoken against their favourite bird should perhaps look away now.)

Even though by April a pair of robins may have been occupying their breeding territory for several months, they must still keep a wary eye out for intruders. And amongst all songbirds, robins are legendary for their aggressive habits.

From time to time, an unmated male or female robin may try to encroach into the territory of an established pair. Even though they do not present an immediate threat, both the incumbent male and female know that these incomers could end up taking over from them later in the season, when they are planning their second brood. So most are given short shrift, and are chased away as soon as they appear.

Now, finally, we realise the purpose of the robin's orange-red breast. In birds, it is quite unusual for both male and female to sport brightly-coloured plumage; normally only the male appears brighter, as almost invariably he takes the leading role in courtship, and needs to woo and convince any visiting females of his qualities as a mate.

Strangely, however, in the case of the robin, in which both sexes look alike, the male's colourful breast is not used for this purpose at all. Instead, it is a warning badge, which tells rival males – and in some cases females – to clear off.

David Lack was the first person to demonstrate this, by means of a very simple – and oft-repeated – experiment. He bought a stuffed robin (for the princely sum of a shilling – 5p in today's money), and placed it strategically inside a male robin's territory, hoping to provoke a response. The first time he did so nothing happened, probably because it was the middle of winter. But the following spring he placed the stuffed robin on a branch just above the nest. Almost immediately, both the cock and the hen began to attack it ferociously.

A few weeks later, when there were chicks in the nest, Lack tried the experiment once again. This time both the cock and the hen immediately tried to drive the intruder away. Their efforts became ever more frantic as, of course, it did not fly off, as a real, live robin would have done. He and others then repeated the experiment at different stages of the breeding cycle, and with different robins. Some virtually ignored the stuffed specimen; others became highly agitated, a few going so far as to peck the bird until feathers were, quite literally, flying.

The next step was to discover whether it was simply the presence of a rival robin (albeit a dead, stuffed one) that so incensed the nesting birds, or something about the colour red itself. Stage by stage, various body parts were removed from the stuffed specimen, until only the red breast was left. Scientists have also tried replacing a stuffed robin with a small piece of orange-red cloth. In both instances, the attacks continued, proving beyond doubt that the robin's colourful breast – which we human beings find so attractive – is the trigger for some of the most aggressive behaviour found in the bird world.

It is often said that robins are one of the very few birds that will fight to the death. That is technically true – on rare occasions they will – but the vast majority of fights between rivals end long before either bird is in any real danger. As Lack wrote in *The Life of the Robin*, 'Just as its song is a war cry, so its red breast is war paint, both song and plumage helping to prevent a fight coming to blows.'

As with other examples of what appears to be naked aggression in nature, such as the black grouse lek or the red deer rut, much of what we see is in effect ritual posturing: a *display* of aggression and power rather than the real thing.

From an evolutionary point of view this makes perfect sense: if every robin went into a fight with the intention of killing or maiming his opponent, then the chances that he might also get injured or killed would dramatically increase.

With my

best Wishes

No bird is earlier awake than the redbreast; it begins the music of the woods, welcomes the dawn of day. It also protracts its warble to the latest hour, and is seen fluttering about in the evening.

Georges-Louis Leclerc, Comte de Buffon,
Histoire Naturelle des Oiseaux, 1771–1786

MAY

One of the most endearing qualities of the robin – apart from its plump, pot-bellied shape and orange-red breast – is its large, black, beady eyes, described by children's author Frances Hodgson Burnett as being 'like black dewdrops'. The eighteenth-century French naturalist Buffon was one of the first to note this, and he perceptively realised that it enabled robins to begin to feed earlier in the morning, and finish feeding later in the evening, than many other small birds.

It's not just the size of the eye – far larger relative to the head and body than ours – that enables them to see well. Robins, like most birds, have very sophisticated eyesight, with a well-developed optic nerve packed with light-sensitive receptors, and the ability to focus through a very wide range: more or less from the tip of their bill to the far distance. They also have very good colour vision, and along with other birds are able to detect light on the ultraviolet wavelength, which we are unable to see. And like all small birds, which are constantly vulnerable to attack by predators, robins have eyes on either side of their head, giving them a very wide field of view.

Good eyesight, and especially a greater sensitivity to low light levels, is essential for a bird like the robin, which mostly forages for its food beneath shrubs and bushes, or under a thick forest canopy, where light levels are far lower than in the open countryside.

Having more time to forage is also a huge asset, especially during the breeding season, when the adult robins need to find food not just for themselves but also for their hungry and ever-demanding chicks. That's especially important for those millions of robins that do not choose to nest in our gardens, where the concentration of natural food and the provision of extra supplies make it relatively easy for them to get enough energy, but instead make their home in woodland.

In a characteristically thoughtful observation, Richard Mabey directly links this physiological aspect of the robin with the deep affection we show towards it:

> Robins' eyes are side-mounted, like most birds; but in that classic robinesque cock of the head, they seem to look directly at us. We're caught in the frankness of that gaze, confronted by an unafraid, unthreatening being as we rarely are by any other creature. No wonder we melt, and feel for a moment that we both live in the same one world.

There are few better places to witness the wonders of a dawn chorus than an English wood, on a fine May Day morning. I've come to a hidden corner of the New Forest, where a patch of ancient woodland plays host to all the expected springtime species: residents, such as wrens, robins, tits and finches; and migrants, including the chiffchaff, blackcap and willow warbler, as well as a few more exotic species, such as redstarts and wood warblers, newly returned from their winter quarters somewhere south of the Sahara.

The sun rises just after 5.30 a.m., but the sky begins to lighten well before that; and an hour or so before dawn breaks the birds begin to sing. It is usually a toss-up between the blackbird and the robin as to which bird will be first off the mark; this morning, to my delight, the robin wins the race. The silence breaks without fanfare, in a slow, measured warble, somewhere in the distance.

As the notes float towards me on the still, early-morning air, the sheer purity of the song is a marvel. Almost immediately a second robin responds, marking out the boundaries of his own territory in response to the first. Although the breeding season is now well underway, male robins must still sing and defend their little patch of ground, for many are already thinking about a second clutch of eggs and a second brood of chicks.

Within minutes, several other robins have joined in, together with the other early birds. These include blackbirds, whose deep, fluty 'oboe-voice' (to quote one Victorian ornithologist) echoes through the foliage; then song thrushes, which sing as if they are telling us a story, with repeated, rhythmic phrases.

Within an hour, the latecomers have started to sing, too: the blackcap, which always sounds to me like a speeded-up blackbird; the willow warbler, whose silvery tones descend the scale like a stream running rapidly downhill; and the urgent, hurried song of the chaffinch, which, as the writer Simon Barnes once noted, sounds like a fast bowler in a game of cricket running into his delivery stride.

Now the whole avian orchestra is singing at full throttle, it is hard to make out the distinctive tones of the robin's song. That may of course be because, having started singing so early, and with the advantage of those huge eyes, which enable it to start feeding a few minutes before the other birds, it has already stopped singing and begun to search for something to eat.

Woodland robins are exactly the same species as our familiar garden birds, though often rather shyer, and also display some other notable changes in their breeding behaviour.

The biggest difference, perhaps, is that they are not resident here: although some robins do remain on and around the woodland edge throughout the year, those that nest deep in the heart of our ancient oak woods usually desert their spring and summer home each autumn. That's because in the middle of winter, in these deep, dark forests, food is thin on the ground and can be very hard to find.

Another important difference between woodland and garden robins is the timing of their breeding season. As you might expect, robins living in gardens usually begin to nest one or two weeks earlier than their woodland cousins, perhaps because of the extra food we provide, which allows them to get off to an early start. Woodland robins cannot rely on a helping hand from us, but they can take advantage of a natural asset: the springtime glut of moth caterpillars, especially in oak woods.

Surprisingly, perhaps, this seasonal abundance of food means that in woods and forests robins breed at a greater density than in suburban gardens; though the highest densities of all are found in hedgerows alongside traditional grassland.

The small green caterpillars that make up the bulk of woodland robin chicks' diet emerge in vast numbers during the spring, and provide a reliable source of energy for many kinds of woodland bird. In Wytham Woods near Oxford, nesting birds are studied more intensively than virtually any other location in the world (by ornithologists based at the Edward Grey Institute nearby). Here, ornithologist David Snow made a bizarre discovery: that the skin of baby robins and blackbirds sometimes turned an odd shade of green – caused by the pigment from the caterpillars that made up the majority of their food.

Back in the garden, the resident robins have already begun to start their second attempt at breeding. Having already paired up much earlier in the year, there is now no need for complex courtship rituals: as long as the weather conditions are OK, and there is enough food, they can simply get on with the process of nest-building and egg-laying once again.

As before, the female does all the hard work building the nest. This time she has chosen a less secluded spot in an elder tree, which could make her more vulnerable to predators. As she passes to and fro with fragments of nesting material, the cock is active too: his job is to carry on feeding the first brood of chicks. They continue to beg for food, just as they did when in the nest; indeed, baby robins will indiscriminately beg from any adult they encounter – a behaviour that generally produces an aggressive response from the unrelated bird.

If it all works out, by the time the female robin has incubated her second clutch of eggs and those chicks have begun to hatch out, the first brood is finally independent, and the male is able to do his duties and feed his new offspring. There is little or no rest for either parent.

By the third week of May the second clutch of eggs has already successfully hatched. Within a few days, once she judges it is safe to leave the youngsters alone for a few minutes, the female again joins the male in his constant efforts to find food for five fast-growing chicks.

The amount of food the adult robins find is truly astonishing, especially as the chicks begin to approach their fledging date. Between them, the cock and hen must bring back up to a thousand separate items every single day. Assuming that towards the summer solstice they are able to feed for fifteen or sixteen hours a day, a quick calculation reveals that each adult must find, catch and bring back a caterpillar, grub or beetle *every two minutes*, from dawn right through to dusk. And remember, they have to feed themselves as well.

At that rate, the feeding procedure becomes almost totally instinctive. As soon as the parent returns to the nest, the chicks go straight into their 'begging mode': opening their bills while uttering a series of loud, high-pitched calls, a behaviour that has evolved to encourage the adults to provide as much food as possible.

But despite their indefatigable efforts, something is wrong. Over the first week or so the chicks grow at a fairly even rate, but as they enter their second week of life it is clear that the smallest chick is failing to put on weight.

It may seem callous, but if this little chick is unable to beg as vigorously as its siblings, its parents will not seek it out to feed it – that would waste precious time, and potentially reduce the chances of their healthier chicks surviving. So as each day passes, the smallest chick gets weaker and weaker, and gradually sinks to the bottom of the nest where, at the age of eleven days, it dies. It could be worse: during cold and wet springs, when bad weather reduces the availability of voles, the larger members in a brood of barn owls may sometimes need to kill and eat their smaller siblings.

Even now, in this fine spring, the other robin chicks are not yet out of danger. The weather can play a crucial role, as it did with the first brood. Extreme weather is the main threat: day after day of rainfall makes it very hard for the adults to find enough food, and if the rain gets really heavy, the female must stop foraging and come straight back to the nest, where she spreads her wings protectively over the chicks to prevent them getting soaked.

Ironically, though, too little rain can be almost as bad as too much. In a long spell of sunny, fine weather the ground becomes very hard, which makes it more difficult for the parents to find insects and other invertebrates. During periods of drought they will sometimes turn to other kinds of food: robins have been seen standing by the edge of shallow pools grabbing minnows and other small aquatic creatures from the water. But mostly they rely on finding a range of insect food and hope that the hot, dry weather soon comes to an end.

On occasion, we humans may ourselves threaten a pair of nesting robins. In May 2004, at the Wyevale Garden Centre in Thornbury, Gloucestershire, an adult robin and two youngsters were killed. But the culprit was not, as you might expect, a cat or sparrowhawk, but a pest control officer.

The reason given for this bizarre and unnecessary act was that old chestnut: 'health and safety'. According to the manager of the garden centre, the birds, which had successfully nested nearby, were causing 'a public health risk' by flying round the cafeteria and perching on chairs and tables. They had also, apparently, set off the burglar alarm by passing through the beam. Such heinous crimes were enough to persuade DEFRA (the Department for the Environment, Food and Rural Affairs) to issue a licence permitting the killing of the robins, which are, like other wild birds, normally protected under the 1981 Wildlife and Countryside Act.

It turned out that this was not the first time such a licence had been issued: during the previous four years, no fewer than nineteen robins had met their deaths through official sanction.

In this particular instance, though, the civil servants and garden centre had both hugely underestimated the public's love of robins, and the outrage such an act was likely to cause. Consumers immediately called for a boycott of Wyevale's business, while conservation and animal welfare organisations spoke with one voice against the killing. The story even made Radio 4's *Today* programme.

As the RSPB pointed out, because the youngsters had already left the nest it was unlikely that they would stay around for more than a couple of weeks, while the RSPCA noted that the health risk to customers was 'vanishingly small'. For Wyevale, it was a case of not so much shooting the bird, as shooting themselves in the foot.

This wasn't the first time that robins venturing indoors have met a grisly end. Writing in the 1850s, the aviculturist William Kidd told of visiting the newly opened Crystal Palace in south London, where to his delight he noticed whole families of tame robins living permanently within the confines of the huge glass building:

> So completely were they 'at home' that here they nested – introducing themselves and their young families at the dinner-table, and going through a whole round of diverting tricks to the infinite amusement of lookers-on.

But a year later, when Kidd and his party made a return visit, he was puzzled to find that there were no robins to be seen, and the whole building 'cruelly silent'. On enquiring as to the birds' whereabouts, to his horror he was told that they had all been poisoned. As he angrily noted, 'Who, after this, shall deny that Man is a Savage?'

In these more enlightened times, I have enjoyed watching robins at large inside the geodesic domes of the Eden Project, near St Austell in Cornwall. Having managed to find their way inside these huge structures, the robins have settled down to a very comfortable life: no predators, no problems with cold or wet weather, and plenty of food on the café tables and amongst the amazing flora growing there. As a result, the Eden robins appear to have become far less aggressive towards one another, with several birds of both sexes happily living side-by-side, with none of the usual antagonism between neighbours that we see outside this cosseted environment.

Back in the garden, roughly two weeks after they hatched, the second brood of young robins is now ready to leave the nest. They do so at a time of plenty: at the end of May there is a glut of food for them to eat, and with just three weeks to go until the summer solstice, plenty of daylight hours for them to find it.

Imagine what it must be like for a young robin, heading out into the big wide world for the very first time. For the first few days of its life it was blind, so its main sensory experience would have been provided by the sound of itself and its siblings begging for food, along with the feeling of being pressed up against each other in the nest.

As it began to open its eyes, it would have seen the sky above: sometimes blue, sometimes grey, sometimes depositing huge drops of very wet liquid, followed swiftly by the comforting arrival of the chicks' mother, whose wings would then protect them from the rain.

By the time the young robin was ready to leave the nest, after two weeks or so, it would have gained a slightly better – though still very limited – understanding of the world around it. Peering out, it would see dense foliage, followed by the more distant greenery of lawns and trees. As it climbed onto the rim, it would look down for the very first time, towards the ground below.

Propelled by a mixture of fear and instinct, it would then make that giant leap into the unknown, to find itself in a far bigger and infinitely more complex world, whose sights and sounds would be at first bemusing, but eventually grow familiar, as it adjusted to its new life outside.

Robins.

After the birds have successfully fledged two broods, you might think both the male and female robins would now deserve a rest. Usually, they get one. But from time to time, if the conditions are right, a pair of robins will attempt to raise a third brood.

As with many songbirds, this partly depends on the geographical location, ideally one with fine, settled weather and a consequent glut of food. Robins in southern Europe regularly raise three broods; those in Scandinavia usually only attempt one; while British robins generally have one or two, and only occasionally three.

For those birds that, having successfully raised eight or nine chicks from two broods to fledging, decline to go through all that hard work yet again, it is finally time to take a rest. Now is the time to try to restore their own energy levels, by finding food just for themselves.

From now on, and throughout the late spring and early summer, I often see the youngsters from the first and second broods as they begin to explore their new – and potentially dangerous – world. Now without the protection from their parents, whose frequent alarm calls are a useful and timely warning of any danger, they may not notice a predator until it is too late.

The youngsters' camouflaged plumage helps them remain inconspicuous. Those speckled, mottled feathers – various shades of buff and brown – blend in very well, especially when they forage for food in the shadows of a hedgerow or shrubbery. But like all robins, the youngsters have a very noticeable, slightly jerky movement, as they hop up and down on our garden furniture, cock their heads and look at me with the same quizzical expression as their parents.

As a young robin stares back at me, I wonder about his chances of survival. It has been calculated, using recoveries of baby robins ringed before they leave the nest, that one in four baby robins will be dead by August, and that three in four will perish by Christmas. That means that, on average, less than a quarter of the robins hatched in my garden will make it through to the following breeding season.

That makes me rather sad; but of course as scientists have pointed out, if even half the youngsters survived to breed, then within a few years we would literally be knee-deep in robins. Like other species, from the long-lived albatrosses that lay just one egg (and, if all goes well, raise one chick) every two years, to the tiniest songbirds that lay several clutches of a dozen eggs, this endearing little bird has evolved to produce more or less the 'right' amount of eggs and chicks, in order to have the best chance of at least one surviving to breed the following year.

Robin Red-Breast

What little birds, with frequent shrillest chirp
When honeysuckle flowers succeed the rose,
The inmost thicket haunt? Their tawny breasts,
Spotted with black, bespeak the youngling
thrush,
Though less in size; it is the redbreast's brood,
New-flown, helpless, with still the downy tufts
Upon their heads.

James Grahame, *The Birds of Scotland*, 1806

JUNE

June is a good month for robins. The weather – Wimbledon fortnight aside – is usually fine, sunny and fairly warm, with less rainfall than earlier or later in the year. Most pairs have by now successfully raised one – and in many cases two – broods of young. And those chicks that have made it as far as fledging are, as the nineteenth-century poet James Grahame perceptively observed, keeping their heads down and out of danger.

There are also plenty of insects available for both the adults and their off-spring to catch and eat. The release from the arduous duties of the breeding season, together with the widespread availability of food, leads to a fascinating change in the behaviour of the breeding pair, which until now have been dedicated in their determination to defend their territory, but now become far more tolerant of their neighbours.

You might think, then, that the male robin would stop singing. After all, keeping up a constant volley of song is very costly for the individual bird. Singing uses up valuable energy, and can also make the bird more vulnerable to attack by a predator as, like other songbirds, robins often sit right out in the open when performing.

So why, now that to all intents and purposes the breeding season is over, does the male continue to sing? The answer lies not in the need to win a mate and repel rival males – the usual reasons why birds sing – but for a third reason: to teach his offspring.

Like other songbirds, baby robins are born with a kind of prototype template in their brains, which contains the basics of their species' song: its rhythm, pitch, tone and so on. Then, to add the finishing touches, they need to listen to their father's song – much as human children learn to speak by listening to their parents.

But experiments in captivity have revealed that if a young male songbird (and in the robin's case, the female too) is not exposed to the song of its father during the crucial period when it is developing from a chick into an adult, then its song is but a poor substitute for the real thing.

That's why, for a brief period after the chicks have left the nest, during the first two weeks or so of June, the male robin in my garden sits out in full view on the top of a hawthorn and sings as if his life depended on it – which, when it comes to the future of his family, it does. Then, having sung more or less continuously since sometime in February, perhaps even earlier, he falls silent. Although his male offspring will begin to sing a few weeks later, towards the end of July, he won't sing again until September.

The robin's sweet and enchanting song is clearly one reason – along with its bright, colourful plumage and endearing tameness – why this species is so well loved, not just here in Britain but in many places. So it's not surprising that robins have been the subject of myths and folklore for many centuries, perhaps millennia. In the ancient Norse religion, for example, the robin was sacred to the god of thunder, Thor, and was supposed to originate in a storm cloud.

Robins also feature in many sayings about the weather. Supposedly, if a robin is singing high in the branches of a tree the weather will be fine, but if it stays low, it will be wet; presumably because if the wind is blowing hard, bringing unsettled conditions, the bird will seek shelter lower down. The great Victorian collector of weather lore, Richard Inwards, unearthed this anecdote from the *Saturday Magazine* of February 1837:

> On a summer evening, though the weather may be in an unsettled and rainy state, he [the robin] sometimes takes his stand on the topmost twig, or on the housetop, singing cheerfully and sweetly. When this is observed, it is an unerring promise of succeeding fine days.
>
> Sometimes, though the atmosphere is dry and warm, he may be seen melancholy, chirping and brooding in a bush, or low in a hedge: this promises the reverse of his merry lay and exalted station.

The same principle, incidentally, applies to swallows, though that has a stronger basis in meteorology, as the flying insects they hunt will generally stay closer to the ground when bad weather is due.

In another observation, though, Inwards noted that the 'long and loud singing of robins in the morning denotes rain'. Such contradictory observations only reveal that most nature-based ways to forecast the weather are at best dubious, and at worst simply wrong.

Perhaps more usefully for our understanding of the deep cultural connection between us and robins, they feature in a wealth of nursery rhymes and children's tales, of which the best known are 'Who Killed Cock Robin?' and 'Babes in the Wood'.

'Who Killed Cock Robin?' first appeared in print as recently as the mid-eighteenth century, in *Tommy Thumb's Pretty Song Book*. Typical of many traditional children's verses – designed to be recited aloud rather than read, and passed down from parent to child for generations – it consists of a series of simple, short, rhyming verses, each of which builds on the previous one to keep the same format:

> Who killed Cock Robin?
> I, said the Sparrow,
> With my bow and arrow,
> I killed Cock Robin.

> Who saw him die?
> I, said the Fly,
> With my little eye,
> I saw him die.

Evidence for the rhyme dating back far earlier than the published version can be found in a fifteenth-century stained-glass window at Buckland Rectory, near Tewkesbury in Gloucestershire, which clearly depicts a robin that has been shot with an arrow.

Like many traditional nursery rhymes, 'Who Killed Cock Robin?' can be read both literally – as the simple story of a bird – and allegorically. Of all the many explanations of its origin and meaning, the most intriguing is that it relates to the death of King William II, the son and heir of William the Conqueror. Known as 'William Rufus' because of his red face, he was killed

Who kill'd Cock Robin?
I, says the sparrow,
With my bow and arrow,
I kill'd Cock Robin.

by an arrow when hunting in the New Forest in the year 1100. Although at the time this was thought to have been an accident, a rumour soon circulated that the (fairly unpopular) king had been assassinated.

For a rhyme supposedly coined for children, 'Who Killed Cock Robin?' does not pull its punches:

> All the birds of the air
> Fell a-sighing and a-sobbing,
> When they heard the bell toll
> For poor Cock Robin.

The children's tale 'Babes in the Wood' also dates back many centuries, and was first popularised as a ballad by the publisher Thomas Millington in 1595. It appeared under the rather unwieldy title 'The Norfolk gent his will and Testament and howe he Commytted the keepinge of his Children to his own brother whoe delte most wickedly with them and howe God plagued him for it' – which mercifully is usually shortened to 'The Norfolk Tragedy'.

The outline of the story is simple. Two small children are abandoned in a wood, where they eventually die. Robins then fly down and cover their corpses with leaves, giving them the equivalent of a Christian burial. As a poignant moral tale for children, it is perhaps not surprising that back in 1932 Walt Disney made it into an animated film, though with a happy ending – in his version, the children do not actually perish.

But delve deeper into the story behind the ballad, and things get rather murkier. According to local legend, the events recounted did actually take place in Wayland Wood in Norfolk, between Norwich and Thetford. The children's uncle is said to have wanted them dead so he could claim their inheritance, and so paid two men to take them into the wood and murder them. But the children were not directly killed but simply left to fend for themselves, and eventually died of starvation. Even today, their ghosts are said to haunt the wood after dark.

The tale became so popular that in 1765 the poet Thomas Percy coined this poignant verse:

> Thus wandered these poor innocents,
> Till death did end their grief;
> In one another's arms they died,
> As wanting due relief;
> No burial this pretty pair
> Of any man receives,

> Till Robin Redbreast piously
> Did cover them with leaves.

The idea that robins cover corpses with leaves may have arisen because, being ground feeders, they are frequently seen in churchyards hopping on and around graves, turning over dead leaves to find food. It is but a short step in the imagination to regard this as the actions of a kindly bird covering up a body. Indeed, one of the many popular books published after the invention of the printing press, Thomas Lupton's 1579 work *A Thousand Notable Things of Sundrie Sort*, noted that 'A Robin redbreast, finding the dead body of a Man or Woman, will cover the face of the same with moss.'

The seventeenth-century poet and cleric Robert Herrick – author of one of the best-known opening lines of any poem in the English language, 'Gather ye rosebuds while ye may...' – also wrote the short verse 'To Robin Redbreast' on the same theme, which I quote in full:

> Laid out for dead, let thy last kindness be
> With leaves and moss-work for to cover me:
> And while the wood-nymphs my cold corse inter,
> Sing thou my dirge, sweet-warbling chorister!
> For epitaph, in foliage, next write this:
> *Here, here the tomb of Robin Herrick is.*

The association of robins with death and burial places remains powerful to this day. In early 2017, a grieving mother, Marie Robinson, was videoing the grave of her young son Jack in Hampshire when she noticed a robin hopping around. Recalling that when Jack was alive he and his twin had always loved robins, she held her hand out – and to her astonishment the bird hopped right up, in full view of the camera.

She later shared her experience on the social media site Facebook, following which the footage went viral, being watched around the world. As Mrs Robinson noted, it seemed that the presence of the robin was a comfort to many people.

It's easy to offer the usual explanation that the robin was probably hoping to find food when it came to her hand. Yet we cannot – and should not – dismiss the huge emotional and spiritual experience of such an encounter, and what it meant to the mother and others who had endured a similar loss.

Although this particular robin – and indeed those featured in 'Babes in the Wood' and Herrick's verse – are suitably kind and thoughtful, reflecting our benevolent attitude towards them, there is a much darker side to robin folklore. As with many other small birds, while we welcome robins in our garden and even on our doorstep, if they cross the threshold into our homes then it is a very different, and far more serious, matter, resulting in the death of one of the inhabitants.

Such dichotomous symbolism – that the robin can represent both good cheer and bad luck – reflects a very profound aspect of our relationship not just with robins, but with the whole of the natural world. Other creatures have their place, and just as long as they keep within their boundaries, and we keep within ours, all is fine. But as soon as they cross over that actual and metaphorical threshold and into our own territory, we tend to respond with hostility and fear. Even our huge love and affection for the robin cannot overcome this.

As well as being illegal under the various bird protection acts to catch and kill a robin, it has also long been considered proverbially unlucky:

The blood on the breast of a robin that's sought
Brings death to the snarer by whom it is caught.

This superstition covers not just adult robins, but also extends to their eggs, as in this traditional nursery rhyme:

The robin and the redbreast
The robin and the wren
If ye take out o' the nest
Ye'll never thrive again.

The robin and the redbreast
The martin and the swallow
If ye touch one o' their eggs
Bad luck will surely follow.

In his popular late-Victorian book *Bird Facts and Fallacies*, the West Country writer Lewis R.W. Loyd recounted many examples of the woe that had befallen people ignorant or rash enough to kill a robin. These ranged from cows producing bloody milk after a Yorkshire farmhand had shot a robin, to another farmer, also in Yorkshire, finding after killing a robin that his entire litter of seven piglets died soon after birth. Even when the pig itself was butchered, the hams it produced went bad. Things then went from bad to worse: the farmer himself died from a fever.

The robin's red breast has also been the source of several other improbable myths. In Wales, children used to be taught that the robin would fill its bill with water from a burning stream in order to try to quench a fire; as a result, the bird acquired a singed breast – and the Welsh name 'Bron-rhuddyn', which means 'breast-burnt'. Children are asked to have mercy on the poor bird and throw it crumbs when it approaches their door. But in a darker tale, if the robin taps three times at the window of a home, then any sick person inside will soon die.

Lewis Loyd's final verdict is that 'the worst that can be recorded of robins is that they are pugnacious to a degree.' Indeed, their reputation for fighting to the death has, he writes, given rise to a belief that as soon as the young robins are strong enough, they will turn on their parents and kill them.

In fact, at this stage of their lives, not only are the youngsters perfectly friendly to their parents, but the intense rivalry we saw earlier in the year between neighbouring pairs of robins also begins to fade away.

Sometimes as early as the end of May, males become less aggressive towards their rivals, and by June two pairs have been watched in the same garden, each collecting insect food for their newly fledged youngsters, without any obvious antagonism between them. However, both hens and cocks will sometimes remain fiercely territorial all the way through June and even July, long after their breeding season has come to an end. Of course, sometimes they do so for a very good reason: the very good years when the weather is fine and there is plenty of food around, and a handful of pairs in Britain attempt to raise a third brood of chicks.

Meanwhile, a pair of sharp, bright yellow eyes is watching one of the newly fledged youngsters from the second brood, as it hops around the lawn and beneath the shrubbery. It is a male sparrowhawk: that paragon of predators, whose entire evolutionary history has turned it into the perfect hunting and killing machine.

At first sight, this appears to be a profoundly unequal contest. The sparrowhawk has powerful wing muscles driving short, rounded wings, and a

Ad. f.   *Juv.*   *Ad. m.*
BRITISH ROBIN   (⅓)   CONTINENTAL ROBIN

long tail – ideal for manoeuvring through the foliage of trees and bushes, as it enables him to twist and turn on a sixpence. The robin is young, small, weak and inexperienced, with little or no defence against attack by its much larger and stronger assailant.

Male and female sparrowhawks have the biggest size difference of any British bird – the females being 25% longer and 75% heavier than their mates. This is for a very good reason. While the bulky female sits on the nest, guarding and warming her eggs and chicks, her smaller and far nimbler mate goes hunting for food, for both her and their chicks. His smaller size and greater agility enables him to specialise in hunting small songbirds – including, of course, robins.

Sparrowhawks have another clever trick up their sleeve. Just as small birds such as robins time their breeding season so that when the chicks hatch there is plenty of food for them to eat – in their case, caterpillars and worms – so sparrowhawks also time the hatching of their chicks to coincide with the greatest availability of food; in their case, newly fledged birds.

This male sparrowhawk's mate began producing her clutch of five eggs in the middle of May, laid two days apart so that one month later the chicks hatch over a period of a week or so. Once they have all emerged, the male really does have to work hard: he must bring back food every couple of hours throughout the day, for at least the next four weeks – that's as many as ten small birds a day, or almost 300 in all.

So you might think, as some have suggested, that sparrowhawks are to blame for the reduction in numbers of some of our commonest songbirds. Yet consider the maths: sparrowhawks are very thinly spread – pairs will rarely nest within less than a kilometre of one another, so that there might be at the most five or six pairs in a square mile.

Within the sparrowhawk's territory there are literally thousands of pairs of small birds – tits, finches, sparrows and robins – each of which may have as many as fifteen or twenty young during the course of a typical breeding season – tens of thousands of baby birds in all. So the chances of any one individual fledgling falling victim to a sparrowhawk are very slim; and overall, the number of chicks taken by sparrowhawks is but a fraction of those that die from other causes.

Finally, as is obvious when you stop to think about it, any predators that managed to wipe out their prey would soon disappear themselves. Sparrowhawks depend on a healthy population of songbirds in their territory; and indeed the presence of sparrowhawks, especially in our towns, suburbs and gardens, is a sign that many garden birds – including the robin – are doing pretty well at the moment.

That doesn't, of course, make it any less upsetting when you witness a sparrowhawk seizing an unsuspecting young bird from your feeders. As

Helen Macdonald, author of the bestselling *H is for Hawk*, has pointed out, when a sparrowhawk kills a bird on your lawn it is as if someone has come into your home and spilled blood over your carpet. We get very possessive about 'our' garden birds, and so when a predator does take one of them we often feel understandably upset, and treat the sparrowhawk as the panto-mime villain of the piece.

But try looking at it from the hawk's point of view. If he fails to catch the small birds it needs to feed his mate and chicks, they will starve to death. And he's as assiduous a parent as the male robin: even after the sparrowhawk chicks have fledged and left the nest they still return to be fed; only after several weeks, once their flight feathers are fully grown, do they finally become independent and hunt for themselves.

And though they might look defenceless, robins and other garden birds do have a few tricks up *their* sleeve. So as the baby robin feeds, happily unaware that it is being watched by the male sparrowhawk, its alert and watchful parent manages to spot the predator hiding in the hedge along the boundary of the garden. Instinctively, the robin utters a sharp '*tic-tic-tic*' call, followed by a soft '*see-ee*', drawing the attention of any bird in the vicinity to the hawk's presence, while trying to stay hidden itself.

Acting on raw instinct, the young robin immediately flies up into a nearby bush to hide away from any danger. The hawk knows the game is up: it too takes flight, pursued as it heads away by the neighbouring swallows, whose own pleasant chattering gains a greater urgency as they see off the predator in the midst. The baby robin has learned an important lesson: unless it becomes more vigilant, keeping a constant eye out for potential threats, it may pay the ultimate price.

Stay, little foolish, flutt'ring thing,
Whither, ah! Whither would you wing
Your airy flight? Stay here and sing,
The mistress to delight.

No, no sweet Robin, you shall not go;
Where, you wanton, could you be
Half so happy as with me?

'Sweet Robin', Anonymous, 1828

JULY

After weeks of typical British summer weather – once cynically defined as 'three fine days and a thunderstorm' – things have settled down at last. The sky is blue, the sun is shining, and yet the garden is more or less silent. Although the blackbird is still feeding chicks in the thick hedgerow, and swallows are still bringing back insects to their second brood in the barn next door, for the vast majority of garden birds – including the robin – the breeding season is over for another year.

So now, for more or less the first time since the turn of the year, I no longer hear the sweet sound of the robin's song when I venture outdoors each morning. Nor do I see a perky little bird foraging for food beneath the shrubbery, or hopping up onto our garden seat, flicking its wings and tail and showing off its red breast. I only occasionally encounter the youngsters, speckled and plump, as they perch on a twig and practise their vocal skills.

I could be forgiven for assuming that all my garden robins have upped sticks and left: migrated, perhaps, or simply hopped over the fence into our neighbours' garden. And yet there are probably more robins around now than at any other time of year. Assuming the adults have survived, along with perhaps two or three youngsters from each of their two broods, then in theory there should be roughly three or four times the number that were here back in January. So where have they all gone?

It's not just robins that have done a disappearing trick. The bird feeders, which only a few weeks ago were thronged with blue and great tits, goldfinches and chaffinches, house sparrows and starlings, are packed with food but empty of birds. Only the collared doves, with their monotonous three-note 'coo-coo-coo', and the slim and dainty pied wagtails perched on our roof, uttering a loud 'chis-ick' call from time to time, break the tedium of a birdless summer's day.

There are two reasons why both the robins and the other garden birds have vanished, and they are connected: food and moult. Most songbirds undergo a change of plumage once a year, and they do so in the middle of summer for four very good reasons.

First, having finished the arduous process of raising a family, they are in a pretty tatty state – if they don't replace their worn-out feathers now, then when winter comes they may not survive. In summer, too, there is plenty of food, and long hours of daylight for them to find it – another good reason to moult now. Moulting can make birds more vulnerable to predators, but in July and August there are plenty of places to hide, as the foliage in our woods, hedgerows and gardens is at its thickest. Having finished breeding, they no longer bear the responsibility of looking after and feeding their own youngsters, which are now fully independent – yet another good reason to moult now.

As the British Trust for Ornithology's Nick Moran has observed on his own local patch in Norfolk, his counts of robins at this time of year fall to roughly half the number he sees from February to April. Soon, having finished their moult, numbers will begin to rise again – helped by the autumnal arrival of migrant robins from further north and east, as well as the population boost provided by this year's juveniles. But as Nick points out, to see robins at this time of year you do need to put in extra effort: now that they have stopped singing and are hiding away out of danger, it is very easy to miss them.

Like other small birds, the adult robin moults its worn-out feathers over several weeks, to ensure that it never loses the ability to fly – essential if it is to be able to feed and flee from any danger. (Ducks, by the way, do lose the power of flight for a week or so, as they moult their flight feathers all at the same time.)

A bird's feathers grow like our hair, from follicles in their skin. That means that, as the new feather grows, it forces out the old, worn one. Overall the whole process can take at least a month, and sometimes as long as two,

during which time a robin will hide away as well as it can, only occasionally venturing out to find something to eat – which is why they seem to vanish at this time of year.

When they do momentarily emerge, you may be shocked to see the state they are in: as they are moulting, adult robins may go almost completely bald, and also lose their long tail feathers, giving them a very odd, stunted appearance. During the period when they moult their breast feathers, of course, they are also unable to fight, and so this time of year sees the lowest levels of aggression between rival birds.

But although they may be vulnerable – especially if the weather turns cool and wet, as it often does during the British summer – as soon as their spanking-new plumage has grown they appear, like models strutting down a catwalk, to show off their finery.

Meanwhile, what has happened to the young birds – this year's juveniles, which left the nest back in May or June and have been feeding avidly to keep up their energy levels, while keeping an eye out for any threats such as cats or sparrowhawks?

They too seem to have disappeared, and that's because they too are moulting. But unlike their parents, which moult all their feathers in one go, young robins undergo what is called a 'partial moult', losing those speckled brown feathers on their breast and back, which are replaced with the classic orange-red breast and brown back of the adult. But they keep their wing and tail feathers for a whole year, only moulting these the following summer.

So if you do see a juvenile robin at this time of year, when they are still moulting, they can look rather peculiar, with hints of orange displacing the brown. But by October, a young robin will essentially look exactly like its parents.

Although many – perhaps the majority – of juvenile robins stay on or around the place where they were born, some do travel farther afield. Three weeks or so after leaving the nest, and becoming completely independent of their parents, some will disperse several kilometres away. Eventually many will fly much farther, travelling more than 100 km (62.5 miles), but will not usually do so until they have moulted into their adult plumage.

For adults and youngsters alike, July is mostly a time to keep their heads down and themselves out of sight. Those living in our gardens have a further hazard to face, especially at a time when they may not be able to fly or manoeuvre themselves out of danger quite so well: cats.

Domestic cats are the scourge of garden birds and other wildlife. The latest survey from the Mammal Society suggests that they are responsible for the deaths of up to 275 million wild creatures every year, of which roughly 55 million are birds. The late Max Nicholson estimated that there are perhaps 120 million breeding pairs of birds in Britain: if you add, say, two young on average for each pair, that means that the maximum number of wild birds, soon after the end of the breeding season, is roughly 500 million individuals. That would mean cats are killing more than one in ten birds every single year.

Another Mammal Society survey, carried out two decades ago, examined the prey brought back by almost 1,000 cats – over 14,000 items in all. Of these, more than 2,800 (about one in five) were birds, of which the robin (with 142 casualties in all) was the fifth commonest (after house sparrow, blue tit, blackbird and starling). The author and naturalist Marianne Taylor has calculated that if these figures were scaled up to cover the whole of Britain, then cats may be responsible for as many as 1.5 million robin deaths every single year.

To put this in perspective, it is fair to say that many of these birds – especially the youngsters and smaller species with a short lifespan – would die anyway before they get the chance to breed again the following spring. Nevertheless, it is still a horrific death toll, and has led to conservation organisations such as the RSPB (many of whose members are cat owners as well as bird lovers) advising people to keep cats indoors, especially at the peak times for hunting, at dawn and dusk, and to hang a bell around their cats' necks to warn birds of their approach.

Some people go much further: in his book *Cat Wars: the Devastating Consequences of a Cuddly Killer*, the eminent US scientist Peter Marra has called for a systematic culling of all feral cats – of which there may be as many as 9 million at large in the United Kingdom, and many more in North America. It might not be popular, but it would certainly make life easier for our garden birds.

One of the most perilous times for a garden robin is when it bathes. Watching a robin bathe in a pond is a real joy: first, it hops tentatively into the water, keeping a beady eye out for any lurking predators. Then it immerses itself, getting an all-over wash by twisting and turning so that the water covers all its feathers, which it ruffles out while shaking its wings to ensure that the liquid gets into every part of its plumage.

Bathing is important for two reasons: it removes the grease and dust from the feathers, and also helps control parasites such as ticks. But it doesn't have to be in water: like other small birds, robins will often sunbathe, spreading out their wings in a sheltered spot in the corner of your garden and feeling the warmth of the sun on their bodies. As with water bathing, though, they need to take care: dozing off can be fatal.

The robin redbreast and the wren
Are God Almighty's cock and hen;
The martin and the swallow
Are God Almighty's birds to hallow.

Nineteenth-century folk rhyme

AUGUST

August is a good month for birds, but sometimes less so for birdwatchers. Plenty of natural food means that birds are able to feed whenever they want; and, having finished breeding, they are far less active than earlier in the summer.

But as the calendar turns inexorably towards autumn, so all birds begin making plans for the season to come – and the winter months beyond. The swallows and martins of that twee Victorian rhyme will soon leave our shores, and head south on their long journey to Africa; while resident birds, such as the robin and the wren, make their own preparations to stay put. They usually stay on or near the territory where they were born back in the spring, or the year before.

As the month goes on, I become increasingly aware of robins wherever I go. I notice one hopping around the edge of a playing field, or on the platform of a railway station while I am waiting for a train. I see them on my local patch, feeding unobtrusively along the edge of the reed bed; and back in my garden, perched on the fence or underneath the hedgerow.

They look smart, as well they might, for their plumage is now immaculate, having moulted their old, worn feathers and grown fresh, new ones. The tail and wings are sleek and neat, the head feathers are no longer sticking up untidily from the crown, and the breast is a full, glorious orange-red – especially when it catches the bright summer sunlight.

From the start of August, through into September, adult robins – both cocks and hens – begin to establish an autumn territory, which they will continue to hold during the next few months until the breeding season begins again early next spring. As David Lack noted:

> From September onwards till May, the woodlands, parks, gardens and hedgerows of England are parcelled out into a great series of smallholdings, each owned by one individual or by a pair of robins. Any robin staking out a territory after September can do so only as a result of the disappearance of an owner or by forcible ejection.

This is make-or-break time for these birds; and not surprisingly, given that the normal population has now been boosted by those surviving young robins looking to find a territory of their own, it's a period of the year when fights between rivals often break out.

For the children's author Frances Hodgson Burnett, whose bestselling story *The Secret Garden* was based on a close relationship she developed with a robin, the idea that such a pretty bird could be so violent came as something of a shock. *My Robin*, published two years later in 1912, opens with an unashamedly anthropomorphic account of her bond with this particular individual in her Kentish garden:

He was an English robin and he was a person – not a mere bird… His body is daintily round and plump, his legs are delicately slender. He is a graceful little patrician with an astonishing allurement of bearing. His eye is large and dark and dewy; he wears a tight little red satin waistcoat on his full round breast and every tilt of his head, every flirt of his wing, is instinct with dramatic significance. He is fascinatingly conceited – he burns with curiosity – he is determined to engage in social relations at almost any cost, and his raging jealousy of attention paid to less worthy objects than himself drives him at times to efforts to charm and distract which are irresistible. An intimacy with a robin – an English robin – is a liberal education.

But the author's affection turns to fascinated horror when a rival male appears in 'her' robin's territory:

He flew at him, he beat him, he smacked him, he pecked him, he shrieked bad language at him, he drove him from the branch – from the tree, from one tree after another as the little traitor tried to take refuge… Perhaps he killed him and left him slain in the bracken… His righteous wrath was awful to behold. I was so frightened that I felt quite pale.

As Burnett witnessed, fights between robins can be surprisingly – and sometimes shockingly – violent. As soon as an incumbent robin spots an intruder it responds immediately, fluffing out its colourful breast feathers in order to look larger and more impressive, and clearly signalling to its opponent that it will not tolerate it muscling in on its patch. Height is also crucial: a robin defending its territory will try to get above its opponent.

Sometimes – indeed, probably on the majority of occasions – this is enough to establish the pecking order and allow the intruder to make a gracious retreat. But not always. The incomer may choose to escalate the conflict by bursting into song, perhaps flying up to an even higher perch as a signal to its rival that it too means business. Now the arms race between the two escalates: the defending robin starts to sing too. Unable or unwilling to retreat, the intruder sings louder and more forcefully; once again, the defending bird does the same.

As with so many conflicts in nature, by now neither bird wants to back down, and a physical fight is almost inevitable. Sometimes this is merely a brief skirmish, in which the owner of the territory readily sees off the rival bird; but if the two are evenly matched, then things can get really violent. The two birds clash, at first using their claws, and then stabbing at one another with that sharp, pointed bill. If one of them manages to get a clean blow to the other bird's head, then the fight may end more quickly than expected, with severe injury or even death.

The ornithologist Bruce Campbell, who knew as much about bird behaviour as most during the post-war era, considered that the killing of one robin by another was unusual, and would only occur in odd circumstances – for example, where two birds were confined in a walled courtyard so neither could retreat or escape. But as the former BTO spokesman Chris Mead once pointed out, the 'murder' of one robin by another is far more common than we used to think: it has been suggested that as many as one in ten deaths are the result of fights between rivals. However, to counter this, despite spending many hours in the field, the great Irish student of robins J.P. Burkitt never actually witnessed a fight to the death himself, suggesting that such encounters may be rarer than we think.

Rob-in.

One of the best accounts of this ferocious behaviour came from a correspondent to an 1884 edition of *The Field* magazine:

> On Sunday last I saw two robins fighting under my dining-room window in such a fierce manner that they astonished me. I watched them until one actually killed the other, and then, like a game-cock, continued to peck his victim. I then went out to examine the poor bird, and found both his eyes out and his skull quite bare...

To his astonishment, however, the winning bird then 'flew onto a branch close to me, and began to sing in the sweetest notes'. But although the contest was over, after singing his victory song the attacker then went back to the corpse of his rival and began pecking violently at it again, making a hole in the dead bird's side.

It is easy for us to moralise about this – especially as the idea that one robin can actually maim or kill another runs so counter to our benign image of this attractive little bird. But we must try not to do so, for the robin's apparently violent behaviour makes complete sense from a biological point of view: these birds have evolved to defend territories both during the breeding season and throughout the autumn and winter.

This puts them on a constant state of alert, and means they can hardly ever let down their guard when a strange robin appears on their home patch. Such behaviour is very different from that of our other garden birds, such as tits and finches, which form communal flocks during the autumn to give them a better chance of finding food in their foraging expeditions.

But there are two major differences between the robin's spring and summer territories, and those it favours in autumn and winter. While during the breeding season the pair defend their joint territory, from now onwards it's every male for himself and every female for herself – autumn and winter territories are owned and defended by a single bird.

The other big difference is size. In autumn and winter a robin's territory is usually considerably smaller in area: a typical breeding territory ranges from roughly 1,600 to over 8,500 square metres, whereas the non-breeding territory ranges from about 700 to 5,000 square metres. The reason is that while during the autumn and winter the territory only needs to provide enough food for one robin, in spring and summer it must support both adults and one or more broods of young.

*　　*　　*　　*　　*　　*

The instinct to fight and drive away a rival to its territory is so great that, from time to time, robins make the mistake of attacking a reflection of themselves in a mirror. David Lack recalled waking one morning to discover that a robin was singing to him – not outside his bedroom, but actually on top of the open window.

What happened next surprised even him: the robin, which had just begun to defend a territory nearby, flew down and began to attack its reflection in the window. Each time it rose up and attacked, so of course the 'rival' matched its movements, driving it into a frenzy. But once it got to the top of the window the reflection promptly disappeared, leading the robin to believe it had won the battle; hence it burst into song.

The robin is not the only bird that attacks its own reflection: pied wagtails, which often frequent car parks, where they hunt for tiny insects on the ground, may mistake a reflection in a car's wing mirror for a rival, and similarly attack it. But given the robin's propensity for fighting off rivals, it's hardly surprising that this is seen more frequently in this species than most others.

One reason why robins are so pugilistic in nature is, as already noted, because they defend a territory all the year round. From late summer onwards they also change their feeding habits – from a spring and summer diet that consists mainly of insects and other invertebrates to an autumn and winter diet where fruit and berries feature far more prominently.

In my own Somerset garden, from late August onwards, the fruit trees reach their peak. As well as a glut of apples – of the eating, cooking and cider-making varieties – there are also crimson haws, ripening blackberries and shiny clusters of honeysuckle fruits. But by far the biggest crop comes from the elders along the hedgerow by the lane, which hang heavy with dense bunches of deep purple elderberries.

Early on a fine morning towards the end of the month, when the dew forming on the lawn hints at the autumn to come, birds begin to gather on the elder to feast on this energy-giving fruit. Since we first moved to Somerset a little over a decade ago, I have recorded more than twenty different species feeding on our garden berry bushes, including such unlikely candidates as great spotted woodpecker, reed warbler and an escaped blue-crowned parakeet, which after being intensely mobbed by the local jackdaws rapidly moved on.

At this time of year, tiny olive-green chiffchaffs move furtively around the foliage, occasionally accompanied by a juvenile lesser whitethroat, refuelling its energy resources before heading on a circuitous migration route to sub-Saharan Africa via the Middle East. But, as you might expect, the most frequent visitors to our berry bushes are the local robins.

In their detailed study *Birds and Berries*, the husband-and-wife ornithologists Barbara and David Snow noted that robins are catholic in their choice of fruit-based food, taking berries from twenty-nine different native species and fifteen introduced ones. In their study area, which spanned parts of Buckinghamshire and Hertfordshire in the Home Counties, they recorded robins feeding on berries in every month of the year except June, when no fruit was available.

As you might expect, numbers peaked in autumn and early winter, with birds starting to switch their diet from insects to fruit in late July and August and continuing through to the following February, after which insect food began to become more widely available once again. The most popular food plants were spindle, whose orange berries are available during the crucial months from November to February; ivy, which likewise fruits very late, and is available all the way through to spring; and elder, which peaks in September but is available from August onwards.

Unlike other birds, which switch their diet from insects to fruit later in the year, the robins observed by the Snows ate more berries – and fed more regularly – during August and September than they did in December and January. Gilbert White, who, as we shall discover next month, was not the robin's greatest fan, made two entries in *The Naturalist's Journal* bemoaning both the consequences of this bird's love of soft fruits:

2nd September 1774: Notwithstanding the prejudices in favour of redbreasts, they do much mischief in gardens to the summer fruits.

10th September 1781: Red-breasts feed on elder-berries, enter rooms, & spoil the furniture.

Whereas thrushes, blackbirds and warblers perch in a bush and feed for a few minutes at a time, methodically working their way through the crop, robins usually snatch a berry in flight, before returning to a nearby perch to consume their booty. They also tend to take smaller items of food than their larger cousins – even blackberries are too big for them to swallow whole.

Watching a robin fluttering momentarily against the lime-green foliage of the elder, before grabbing a berry and flying off, I am reminded of the extraordinary process of symbiosis I am witnessing. It's easy to imagine that the bird gets all the advantages here: an ample and convenient supply of tasty and nutritious food. But of course the plant benefits too: indeed, it has evolved the ability to wrap its seeds in strikingly coloured, fleshy fruit in order to spread them far and wide.

Soon after the robin has fed to its heart's content, it will fly away, and then eventually defecate, spreading the elder's tiny seeds where they can germinate and grow. In a year or two, this robin's offspring may be feeding on berries from a plant that is only alive thanks to its parent's love of that juicy purple fruit.

August also sees the start of the football season – another indication that, despite the sweltering heat, autumn and winter are not too far away. Supporters of no fewer than four Football League and four non-league teams may shout out 'Come on the Robins!' to encourage their side. (Indeed, the only nickname that beats this, with nine clubs in all, is the far less imaginative 'the Blues'.) It may not surprise you to learn that Bristol City, Charlton Athletic, Cheltenham Town and Swindon Town, who all play in a predominantly red

ERITHACUS RUBECULA Lin
Rödhake.

strip, have an association with our bird, as does the rugby league team Hull Kingston Rovers.

The nickname 'Robin' – as we've seen, originally derived from the more formal Robert – has also become a common Christian name. Robert, a name widely found in various forms across much of Europe and the rest of the English-speaking world, was originally a Germanic name meaning 'bright fame'.

The affectionate diminutive 'Robin' seems to have arisen during medieval times: the first known reference comes from the late fourteenth century, from the poem *Piers Plowman*, and soon afterwards it also appears in Chaucer's *Troilus & Criseyde*.

Of course, the best-known Robin of all was the legendary hero of Sherwood Forest, Robin Hood, celebrated in rhymes, stories and latterly in major Hollywood movies for stealing from the rich and giving to the poor.

An even more intriguing 'Robin' appears slightly later on, first in the writings of the reformist Protestant scholar William Tyndale, in 1528, and then in Shakespeare's *A Midsummer Night's Dream*, written during the 1590s. 'Robin Goodfellow' is an alternative name for that mischievous sprite Puck, a hobgoblin that lulls people into a false sense of security by tidying up or doing their housework, and then undoes his efforts by 'knavish tricks' and practical jokes. A popular literary character throughout the seventeenth century, referred to by, amongst others, Ben Jonson and John Milton, he appears to have fallen out of favour soon afterwards, and is rarely heard of today.

There are still, however, a number of phrases and compound words derived from the bird name robin. These include 'robin-in-the-hedge', used for a range of creeping plants such as ground ivy and cleavers – which presumably derives from the robin's habit of skulking low along the ground. Common woodland and hedgerow plants with red flowers may also have a robin-based nickname: they include red campion ('robin-flower'), the cranesbill geranium or herb robert ('red robin') and a plant found in wet meadows and pastures, ragged robin.

Rose galls – those unusual spiky objects found on wild rose plants – are often known as 'robin's pincushions'. They are in fact caused by a small insect, the gall wasp, laying its eggs in the unopened buds, which instead of flowering go on to develop a striking appearance and reddish colour – hence the name.

Robin's-egg is also often used to describe a pale blue shade: confusingly, though, this comes from the colour of the egg of the larger American robin; European robins' eggs are of course not blue, but creamy-white with reddish speckles.

Perhaps the oddest use of the word 'robin' in English is the now obsolete phrase 'Robin's Dinner'. Dating from the late Victorian era, it refers to a free meal provided for destitute children at Christmas by charitable donors. As one contemporary account, written in 1877, noted: 'Robin succeeded so well last year… that his Christmas thoughts are becoming very expansive, and he now wants to establish "A Robin Dinner" for waifs and strays everywhere.' This must have continued well into the twentieth century, for as recently as 2006 the *Lincolnshire Echo* newspaper referred to the revival of 'the old Robin Dinner… once a highlight of the year for many Lincoln children'.

DAVID LACK

The Life
of the Robin

A full account of Britain's most popular bird written primarily for the
layman and illustrated with line
drawings and photographs

2/6

Where are the songs of Spring? Ay, where are
they?
  Think not of them, thou hast thy music too –
While barrèd clouds bloom the soft-dying day,
  And touch the stubble-plains with rosy hue:
Then in a wailful choir the small gnats mourn
  Among the river sallows, borne aloft
    Or sinking as the light wind lives or dies;
And full-grown lambs loud bleat from hilly
bourn;
  Hedge-crickets sing; and now with treble soft
  The red-breast whistles from a garden-croft;
    And gathering swallows twitter in the skies.

John Keats, from 'To Autumn',
written 19 September 1819

SEPTEMBER

Dawn comes later now – so late that my alarm clock often goes off before the light coming in through the bedroom curtains awakens me, starting my day in a most unwelcome manner.

But this morning I wake before the dreaded bleep, to an altogether more pleasant sound: the song of a robin. I am hearing him for the first time in more than two months, since he last serenaded his mate and their second brood of almost full-grown chicks for a few weeks in June, soon after they had left their nest.

I lie listening to what sounds like the familiar voice of an old friend, a sound I didn't expect to hear, yet which makes perfect sense. It also reminds me that time is passing, and that although summer is still with us, autumn will soon begin, with winter just around the corner.

The older I get, the more I find myself attuned to the tiny changes that occur in nature from week to week and even day to day, which together mark the changing of the seasons. None of them are notable in themselves but, like the second hand ticking on a clock, they accumulate into major shifts in time – and, in the case of the natural world, space. The robin's September song is one such natural indicator.

Later that day, walking down the road into my village, I can hear several robins, each of which is marking out its territory from the next in an orderly but definitive way, with its autumnal song. On the telegraph wires outside the local shop, Keats's 'gathering swallows' are preparing for departure. Like impatient travellers in an airport terminal, they are fidgety and restless, every now and then leaving *en masse* and skimming around the skies, twittering noisily, before returning to their place.

One day soon – sometime around the middle of the month – they will leave their perch and swoop up into the September sky for the very last time. Instead of returning, they will fly away from our little Somerset village, heading across the English Channel, through France, over the Mediterranean Sea and the Sahara Desert, crossing the Tropic of Cancer, the Equator and the Tropic of Capricorn, before finally reaching their destination: the Cape of Good Hope in South Africa. It will be six months before we hear their twittering calls again, in early April next year.

But for the robins, which pour out their song with all the energy they can muster, there are no such global wanderings. Their destiny is not to travel the world, but to stay put, right here in this West Country village. And that, of course, is why they are singing: for, as we have already seen, robins are one of the very few British birds that defend a territory not just in spring and summer, when breeding, but throughout the autumn and winter too.

They do so not to fend off rival males and attract females, as in spring, but simply to mark off a small area where they can rely on finding food, every single day for the rest of the year and beyond. Small birds in winter face a simple but life-or-death problem: if they don't get enough to eat – every single day – they will die.

Most birds follow a more sociable strategy: the blue and great tits that nested alongside the robins earlier in the year now form into flocks, which rove around gardens, parks and woods like a gang of teenage tearaways. They call excitedly to one another when they find food, and happily share it with their peers – which may also include hangers-on such as goldcrests, treecreepers and long-tailed tits.

But robins – true to their belligerent nature – don't do sharing. As the third-century BC Greek philosopher Zenodotus noted, 'One bush does not shelter two robins'. Instead, they have chosen the solitary path, which means holding a territory against any intruders, which they do by singing. This also explains a curious phenomenon: that at this time of year, uniquely amongst British birds, female robins also sing.

I say 'uniquely', even though female wrens, dunnocks and dippers do occasionally sing, while some African species of shrike duet with one another, the male singing one part and the female the other. But the robin is the only bird in which we hear the female singing so regularly – indeed scientists have observed that in autumn females may even be more vocal than males. So the robin in Edward Thomas's verse – that 'sings over again, Sad songs of Autumn mirth' – might actually have been a hen bird.

Because male and female robins are so similar in appearance that we cannot tell a bird's sex simply by looking at it, it was less than a century ago that female robins were discovered to sing. The man who did so was the esteemed Irish ornithologist J.P. Burkitt, who carried out detailed field studies of robins in his garden in the town of Enniskillen, County Fermanagh. He managed to do so entirely in his spare time, while continuing his day job as the County Surveyor, introducing the first tarmac roads to this part of Ireland.

Born in 1870, James Parsons Burkitt did not even develop an interest in birds until he was in his late thirties. Yet he soon made up for lost time, becoming one of the most influential amateur ornithologists Ireland has ever produced. He observed robins more intensively, and for longer periods, than anyone had ever done before, and arguably (David Lack notwithstanding) since, and published his ground-breaking observations – including the hitherto unknown fact that female robins sing – in *British Birds* magazine between 1924 and 1926.

Having taken up bird ringing in 1922, Burkitt ringed one female robin on 18 December 1927, and then trapped it again more than a decade later, in July 1938, making the bird at least eleven years old. This is still a UK record for this usually short-lived bird – the oldest robin ever found in Britain was re-trapped a mere eight years and five months after it was first ringed. (There are two European records of robins surviving even longer: seventeen years and three months, from Poland, and an astonishing nineteen years and four months, from the Czech Republic.)

Burkitt lived to the ripe old age of eighty-eight, dying in 1959. So he survived to see his work championed by Lack, who was an ardent admirer of this pioneer in the study of bird behaviour. In his Preface to the fourth edition of *The Life of the Robin* (published in 1965, six years after Burkitt's death), Lack paid tribute to this modest, deeply religious man:

> Apart from his strikingly original work on the robin, begun after the age of fifty, he published almost nothing, perhaps because... 'I had pricks of conscience that I was really more interested in the created than the Creator.'

According to Lack, Burkitt spent his last years reading the Bible and culti-
vating his garden – no doubt accompanied by his beloved robins.

Both Burkitt and Lack observed, as have many careful listeners, that the autumn song of both male and female robins differs subtly in tone from the
one we hear in spring. It is softer, quieter and, some would say, more plaintive and melancholy, perhaps reflecting our own feelings as summer slips
away. The poet Robert Burns concurred, writing of the robin's 'pensive autumn cheer'.

However, applying human emotions to birdsong opens a Pandora's Box
of questions about our human response to nature. All we can definitively

say is that there is no evidence that the other robins, for which the song is produced, hear it that way.

There is a problem, however, with the traditional hypothesis that the reason both male and female robins sing and defend a territory in autumn and winter is exclusively to do with food. After all, early autumn is, as Keats noted, the season of 'mellow fruitfulness': a time of plenty, when food resources are at their highest, with plenty of berries, seeds and insects on which the birds can feed. So surely there is no need for any robin to waste precious energy singing to defend a small patch of land against rivals?

David Lack himself was well aware of this conundrum:

> Clearly the autumn territory has no value in pair-formation or any other breeding behaviour, since the robin does not normally breed in autumn. It might therefore be supposed that it can only be a food territory. But there are considerable objections to this view. Food trespassing is regular, possible food competitors of other species are not driven out, and the size of the autumn territories is even more variable than that of the spring ones. Further, territorial fighting is most vigorous during August and September, when food is abundant, and wanes in November and December, when food is getting scarcer.

There are several possible solutions to this puzzle. One is the simple observation that on fine days in autumn quite a few songbirds sing – I have often heard wrens, dunnocks and chiffchaffs in full song in September. It may be that the similarity between spring and autumn – when the length of the day in particular is almost the same – might simply be fooling some birds into thinking spring has come around again, and so they start to sing and hold territory.

The downside of this explanation is that both hen and cock robins sing and defend a territory at this time of year, and indeed do so far more systematically and consistently than any other species.

So why do both male and female robins sing so persistently during the autumn and winter? True to his innate curiosity, Lack came up with another, rather ingenious, solution: that, being a partially migratory species, some robins sing at this time of year in order to suppress their innate instincts to migrate. So instead of heading away from their breeding territories – which, as we shall soon see, many robins do – they stay put, singing their hearts out. By fooling themselves into thinking that the breeding season is about to start, in other words, they are prevented from following any latent migratory instinct and flying south. It's a clever theory, but I have to say I'm not entirely convinced.

Meanwhile, the robin continues to sing outside my bedroom window, and will carry on doing so for the next few months. I may be wrong to take delight in what is, after all, a purely biological phenomenon. Yet as I lie in that half-world between sleep and waking, the sweet, sad notes of the robin's September song percolating into my consciousness, I cannot help feeling good about the day ahead. Thus does nature sustain and fulfil us, often in the most unexpected and delightful ways.

So what of another unusual aspect of the behaviour of robins: that they are frequently heard singing in the middle of the night?

As a student at Cambridge, almost forty years ago, I recall walking home one autumn night, well after I should have been tucked up in bed. To my surprise, as I reached my college, I heard the unmistakable sound of a singing robin, bursting out into the otherwise silent night, as loud and clear as on a fine spring morning.

I thought little more about this until many years later when I was producing an episode of the TV series *The Nature of Britain*, on wildlife in cities. My researcher came up with new findings suggesting a reason why robins – and indeed some other songbirds – habitually sing at night. Bear in mind that we are not talking about singing in the hour or so before dawn, which is commonplace; or even as night falls, which is certainly regular; but rather a full-blown nocturnal performance.

In the past, some scientists have suggested that birds – especially those in cities – sometimes sing during the night as it is quieter than during the day, when they have to compete with the usual noises from people and traffic. But although there may be some truth to this – after all, it is thought that nightingales sing at night to avoid being drowned out by other birds – the real reason turns out to be to do with that beady black eye.

As we know, the robin has a disproportionately larger eye, compared to its head and body size, than many other birds, enabling it to forage for food in dark places at dawn and dusk. But researchers at Glasgow University have discovered that this also makes robins sensitive to certain wavelengths of light – especially the blue light emitted by neon signs.

Because of this, the birds' body clock is being disrupted by the prevalence of artificial light in cities, causing them to assume that dawn has broken and it is time to sing. It gets worse. Once one robin starts singing, this acts as a signal to neighbouring robins to sing, too, to defend their own territory. Thus once one bird has woken up, they all do.

The scientist leading the research, Dr Davide Dominoni, believes that as a result many urban robins are exhausted, leading to weakness and presumably hastening the chances of an early grave. He has suggested modifying street lamps to reduce light pollution, which hopefully might discourage the robins from staying up and singing all night.

Although the robin's habit of singing through the night may be on the increase, thanks to the increase in light pollution, it has clearly been going on longer than we might think: in his 1869 novel *Lorna Doone*, R.D. Blackmore noted that 'Everyone knows that robins sing all night'. This nocturnal singing may even have been the inspiration for the Second World War song 'A Nightingale Sang in Berkeley Square': and confusion between these two nocturnal singers still occasionally rears its head.

When Margaret Thatcher was Prime Minister it is said that she breezed into a meeting one morning and announced that the night before a nightingale had serenaded her from just outside the window of 10 Downing Street. When a civil servant hesitantly suggested that nightingales are summer visitors to Britain, and would already have left for Africa, she insisted that her identification of the bird had been correct.

But nightingales are rural birds, persisted the hapless adviser, and even if one had stayed behind instead of migrating it would not be here in Central London. Still the Iron Lady demurred.

The official was about to contradict her for a third time when his boss leant quietly over and hissed in his ear, 'If the Prime Minister *says* she heard a nightingale, she heard a nightingale!'

Given that the robin is one of the very few birds that sing regularly through-out the autumn, it is not surprising that poets and naturalists through the ages have referred to this unusual habit.

One of the first to do so was the eighteenth-century parson-naturalist Gilbert White, whose *A Natural History of Selborne* became the best known – and for many readers the best loved – of all classic nature writings. Yet White was himself ambivalent about the robin's autumn song, as can be seen from this journal entry from 1776: 'The redbreast's note is very sweet and pleasing; did it not vary with it ugly associations of ideas, and put us in mind of the approach of winter.'

Writing half a century later, in the poem 'September 1819', William Wordsworth took a more positive view, though with a tinge of melancholy:

> No faint and hesitating trill,
> Such tribute as to winter chill
> The lonely redbreast pays!

But for a tribute that sums up our closeness to the robin, reinforced by its habit of singing throughout the darkest months of the year, the early nine-teenth-century poet and schoolmaster Noel Thomas Carrington takes some beating. Addressing the robin as 'sole minstrel of the dull and sinking year', Carrington also celebrates its famous tameness:

> Sweet household bird! That infancy and age
> Delight to cherish, thou dost well repay
> The frequent crumbs that generous hands bestow;
> Beguiling man with minstrelsy divine,
> And cheering his dark hours, and teach him
> Through cold and gloom, autumn and winter, Hope.

But for some robins, the delights of an English garden are still very far away, as they contemplate a long, hazardous and potentially fatal journey across the North Sea. More than any other aspect of this bird's life, this reminds me of David Lack's conclusion to a lifetime's study of the species:

> The world of a robin is so strange and remote from our experience that into it we can scarcely penetrate, except to see dimly how different it must be from our own.

Sweet little bird in russet coat
The livery of the closing year
I love thy lonely plaintive note
& tiney whispering song to hear
While on the stile or garden seat
I sit to watch the falling leaves
The songs thy little joys repeat
My lonliness relieves
& many are the lonely minds
That hear & welcome thee anew

John Clare, 'The Autumn Robin', 1835

OCTOBER

So far, it has been a dry, and surprisingly warm autumn. What rain there has been has usually fallen in short cloudbursts, overnight, so that the days have been fine and mostly sunny.

For those of us keen to see migrant birds as they head south, it has been a quiet autumn, at least where I live, near the west coast. At this time of year keen birders pray for bad weather, which brings the birds down to land along our coasts; whereas these fine conditions mean they simply fly straight over on their long journey south. So, apart from a few wheatears hopping about the sea wall near Burnham-on-Sea, and the odd whinchat perched upright on the hawthorn like a sentinel, this autumn has been more or less migrant-free.

So when I hear a repetitive ticking from the same hedgerow, a hundred metres or so back from the coast, I don't think much of it. Then, realising that it is a robin, I decide to take a look. The sound is coming from the base of a rhyne, the water-filled ditch that runs alongside the track. I wait expectantly for the bird to show itself, yet it fails to do so. The robins here are usually as exhibitionist as they are everywhere, hopping up onto the grass or the twig of a bush; but this one remains resolutely hidden. Nor does it, as again I would normally expect, burst into song.

Eventually I head back to my car; but then it dawns on me that this bird could be behaving oddly for a good reason. It may not be one of our resident robins, staying put on its permanent territory. Instead it is likely to be a continental bird, passing through Somerset on its way south.

Just like the wheatears and whinchats I saw a week or so ago it is a migrant, and although it will not complete such an epic journey as theirs, all the way to Africa, it will nevertheless travel a fair distance. It has already flown here across the North Sea from its breeding grounds in Scandinavia, and will soon depart, to spend the winter in France or Spain, or perhaps as far away as North Africa.

Years ago I was walking out to Blakeney Point, that long spit of shingle that sticks out into the North Sea parallel with the north Norfolk coast, a famous hotspot for migrants. Trudging out towards the end was like wading through porridge, and when we finally reached the point itself we had to sit down to recover our breath.

After a few minutes, I noticed a bird hopping from a low bush down onto the ground in a very familiar manner. It was, of course, a robin; indeed, there were several of them, but like my Somerset bird they weren't behaving in the way I would expect. Far from being tame and confiding, they were wary and secretive, only occasionally emerging from the thick cover of thorns. They looked different too: sleek and slender, not plump, with – though this was perhaps a trick of the autumn light – paler orange breasts.

These, without any doubt, were continental robins; immigrants that had flown overnight from Scandinavia, taking advantage of high pressure and following winds to hop across to Britain on the first leg of their journey south and west. As dawn broke they had made landfall here, and would now rest and feed by day before heading off again that evening, under cover of darkness.

That day in Norfolk, I came across only a few robins but, given the right weather conditions, huge flocks may sometimes be seen. In 1637, the Puritan dissenter Dr John Bastwick was convicted of preaching seditious sermons, having denounced bishops as enemies of God. After having his ears cut off and being fined the then enormous sum of £5,000 (roughly £500,000 today), he was exiled to Star Castle on the Isles of Scilly: then, as now, a hotspot for migrating birds. His friend William Prynne later recorded that:

> Many thousands of robin redbreasts (none of which birds were seen in those islands before or since), newly arrived at the Castle there the evening before, welcomed him with their melody, and within one day or two after tooke their flight from thence, no man knows whither.

This was the first recorded example of continental robins passing through Britain on their way south. But it was certainly not the last: on 1 October 1951 birdwatchers along the whole of Britain's east coast witnessed what came to be known as the 'Great Robin Rush', as huge numbers of migrant robins appeared at watch points from Fair Isle in the north to Kent in the south.

The figures were staggering: keen bird ringers managed to trap and ring well over a thousand birds: 300 at the Isle of May off the coast of Fife, and 500 each at Spurn in East Yorkshire and Gibraltar Point in Lincolnshire. Given that ringed birds represent only a small fraction of the total number – many of which would have passed overhead by night, unseen – we can only speculate that the total numbers involved would have been in the tens of thousands, perhaps even more. As always with the ringing of songbirds, however, only a tiny proportion were recovered: just five of the birds ringed at Spurn Bird Observatory, which were found in Menorca, France and Italy.

The reason for this unprecedented arrival of robins was the particular weather conditions that occurred over the days leading up to the sightings. The birds would have left Scandinavia on the last day of September, in near-perfect conditions: a stable high-pressure system bringing clear skies, and a cool breeze. This allowed them to set their course using the moon and the stars, and the Earth's magnetic field.

But as they headed out over the North Sea, the weather started to change very rapidly. Cloud began to form over Denmark, and during the course of the night a thick bank of fog appeared, disorienting the birds – many of which would have been birds born earlier that year and on their very first migratory journey.

Confused and exhausted, and with their normal navigational tools rendered useless by the cloud and fog, many of these inexperienced robins would have fallen into the waves. But for some, one other aspect of this particular weather system proved their saviour. Easterly and north-easterly winds began to pick up speed, pushing the birds off their normal course and allowing them to make landfall on the east coast of Britain. As dawn broke, the bushes along coastal headlands and islands teemed with robins. Never has such a concentration of robins been witnessed before or since.

We don't usually think of robins as migrants, and indeed, John Bastwick's sighting and the 'Great Robin Rush' notwithstanding, the vast majority are not. Studies of the movements of ringed birds have revealed that only a tiny number – perhaps one in thirty – travel more than 20 kilometres (12.5 miles) from their birthplace; while coloured rings placed on robins have also shown

that most males hold territories which actually overlap with the one where they were born a year or two before.

Yet some robins do migrate. A small number of British robins (of the race *melophilus*) – perhaps five per cent, almost all females and juveniles – leave our shores each autumn and spend the winter on mainland Europe, mostly in northern France. However, ringed birds have also been found as far south as Spain and Portugal, with one bird – ringed as a young bird in Montgomeryshire in Wales – flying more than 1,600 km (1,000 miles) to south-west Spain. Sadly, having made all that effort, it was then shot by a trigger-happy hunter.

Meanwhile, continental robins – of the nominate race *rubecula* – start appearing from late August onwards, usually along the east coasts of England and Scotland. They can be seen as late as November, though the peak numbers make landfall here in October. Interestingly, soon after numbers of new arrivals peak along our east coast they begin to filter inland: in mid-October 2014 a fall of ninety robins recorded at Scolt Head, Norfolk, was followed just a couple of days later by a huge increase in robin numbers – from just four birds to twenty-eight – at the BTO's headquarters near Thetford, over 40 miles inland.

These migrant robins are mostly from Scandinavia – as far north and east as Finland – but recoveries of ringed birds have revealed that some come from eastern Europe, the Baltic states or the Low Countries. They will travel as far south as the Iberian Peninsula or even north-west Africa, most heading onwards within a day or two of their arrival here.

However, a few of these continental robins do occasionally stay put in Britain for the whole of the winter. That shy, pale, nervous-looking robin skulking beneath your garden shrubbery may have travelled further than you think.

It is almost impossible to imagine what it must be like to be a migrant bird. How must it be to embark on an epic journey across the sea, barely a few months after hatching out of a tiny egg, naked, blind and helpless?

Yet that is exactly what robins do when they leave their birthplace in Scandinavia and head south and west to spend the winter in Britain. Like all migrants – especially those birds born earlier in the year, which are flying south for the very first time – they are driven by a combination of instinct and a response to the particular weather conditions they encounter *en route*. Success is a matter both of luck and judgement, and many fail to survive this, their very first journey.

*   *   *   *   *   *

Let us try to picture the scene, at dusk on a fine, dry evening in the middle of October, somewhere the other side of the North Sea. Earlier in the day, a weak weather front crossed slowly from west to east, bringing light showers. But now that the front has passed, the barometer is starting to rise, and the air temperature is beginning to drop – a sure sign that an area of high pressure is moving in.

Something in the tiny brain of this young robin – and his companions – is telling him that the time has come to depart. The days have been shortening and, although he has been feeding avidly to build up weight, finding food has become harder and harder. Fortunately, coming across a lush crop of ripe hawthorn berries has allowed him to increase his fat reserves, and, having moulted a few weeks ago from his speckled juvenile plumage into the orange-red, grey and brown finery that marks him out as a mature robin, he is ready to depart.

Like almost all songbirds – apart from swallows and martins, which feed on the wing while travelling – robins migrate by night. They do so for several very good reasons: the air is cooler, producing less resistance and allowing them to maintain their body temperature; the cover of darkness keeps them safe from predators; and once they do reach landfall, they can rest and feed during the day before setting off on the next leg of their travels.

Now, an hour after sunset, the conditions are ideal, with clear skies and light north-easterly winds. In response to some unseen signal, the robin launches himself into the air, and heads off.

For many millennia, our ancestors would marvel at the miracle of migration – although some ancient philosophers refused to countenance the idea at all. In the fourth century BC, the Greek philosopher Aristotle suggested an alternative theory – that of transmutation – in which birds simply turned from one species into another. Famously, he believed that in winter the redstart, a summer visitor to Greece, changed into a robin. This mistake persisted for almost two thousand years, until in the middle of the sixteenth century the pioneering English ornithologist William Turner finally disproved it beyond any reasonable doubt.

Even today, now that we know how birds navigate across the surface of the globe, we are still filled with awe. Unlike human navigators, who tend to rely on maps and memory – and nowadays computer satnav systems – birds use a whole toolkit of different methods to help them find their way.

The earth's magnetic field is key: experiments with captive birds have shown that when the polarity of their surroundings is altered, they instinctively head in what should be the right direction, even when this is 90 or 180 degrees out of line with the actual one. Like ancient sailors, they also use the stars – and at dawn and dusk, the position of the sun, or on cloudy days, polarised light. As they get nearer to their destination they will follow geographical features such as coastlines or rivers; and on their return spring journey, when very close to home, they may even recognise specific landmarks.

But for this little robin, the first challenge is to cross the vast expanse of the North Sea. This is where instinct must take over, with the bird choosing a course and then trying to stick to it. But just because the weather is good at his starting point, does not mean it will be at his destination, or along the way. There may be high pressure over Scandinavia, but farther south, the weather is very different indeed. A low-pressure system is bringing strong headwinds, cloud and rain, making it impossible to see the stars, and indeed hard to see at all.

Still the robin pushes on, impelled by instinct to reach land. He has been flying for many hours, and a glow to his left signals that dawn is beginning to break in the east. The rain is becoming torrential, and his energy reserves are dwindling. But generations of evolutionary adaptation now begin to kick in: he is only here because his parents, grandparents and previous ancestors back through history survived this perilous journey. If he fails at this stage, that lineage is over forever.

In the far distance, somewhere towards the right-hand side of his vision, something flashes. A light; and then again, and again. Something tells him to head in that direction, and as he does so the light gets stronger and stronger, still pulsing at regular intervals, every few seconds. Finally, it is so bright the robin thinks that dawn must have suddenly broken, yet moments later he is plunged into darkness, then light once more. Mesmerised, he continues to head towards the regular flashes; but at the last moment something warns him not to get too close, and he folds his wings and drops downwards.

Then he sees the ground coming up towards him at speed. He instinctively brakes and, moments later, lands on a soft grassy sward. Looking around, he can see a dense hawthorn hedgerow, into which he dives. Listening above the gently falling rain, he can hear the gentle ticking of other robins, the alarm call of a blackbird, and other bird sounds. He is safe – for the time being, at least.

The flashing light was, of course, a lighthouse: the one standing proud on the top of Flamborough Head, on the Yorkshire coast between the holiday resorts of Bridlington and Scarborough. This rocky promontory sticks out into the North Sea – indeed, the name 'Flamborough' may come from the Anglo-Saxon word for dart, as the headland does look rather like the head of an arrow.

The lighthouse was originally built in the early nineteenth century, to provide a warning to passing ships of the position of the promontory. But since then, it has been both the salvation and the destroyer of migrating birds. Some,

like this robin, are able to use the light to guide them in towards the safe haven of land; others crash right into the glass around the flashing light. Each morning, at the bottom of the lighthouse, there are sad little lifeless corpses, their journey having ended prematurely just when they should have been safe.

Today, this robin is one of the lucky ones. He has managed to cross the North Sea, by far the greatest hazard on his voyage. Now, after recovering from the rigours of his flight, he will feed quietly on the ground beneath the hedgerow, before snatching a few hours of sleep. The next night, he will set off again; this time on a much shorter and easier journey, to a woodland or garden somewhere in southern England. There he will spend the rest of the autumn and winter, alongside our resident robins, before heading back north and east next spring, to breed for the very first time.

★ ★ ★ ★ ★ ★

As soon as we get out of the car, the first thing I hear is a robin singing – a good omen. For I am on a pilgrimage. This is Dartington Hall in Devon, the rambling, wooded country estate near Totnes where, more than 80 years ago, David Lack began his lifelong study of robins.

Today, Dartington is best known for its summer school and annual literary festival, 'Ways with Words', which attracts leading fiction and non-fiction authors from all over Britain and beyond. Last time I was here, giving a festival talk, my paltry audience was far outgunned by the Booker Prize-winning author of *Wolf Hall*, Hilary Mantel, whose queue of hundreds of eager fans snaked all the way around the main house.

Today things are a little quieter, though, it being half-term, the car park is still full, there are ramblers wearing brightly coloured waterproofs, and there is a wedding taking place – one of the many ways country estates such as this keep their head above water in tough financial times.

The Dartington Estate dates back to at least the ninth century, while the hall itself was built from 1386 onwards by John Holland, the Earl of Huntingdon and half-brother of the reigning King, Richard II. After Holland was beheaded in 1400, for treason towards Richard's successor, Henry IV, the house eventually passed into the hands of a noble family, the Champernownes. But by the 1920s the hall had become derelict, and was in danger of falling down.

It was saved by an extraordinary couple, Leonard and Dorothy Elmhirst. Using the American-born heiress Dorothy's fortune, they restored the house and grounds and embarked on a radical experiment in communal living – a kind of pre-hippy community, devoted to progressive education, sustainable employment, rural renewal, culture and the arts.

It was into this setting that the twenty-three-year-old David Lack arrived in late 1933, as a newly appointed biology master at the recently opened school. In some ways this was an odd choice for this young man: he had enjoyed a comfortable and fairly conventional upbringing, the eldest son of a distinguished medical physician and his wife, a former actress. Educated at Gresham's School in north Norfolk, the young David had developed an early interest in birds – a lifelong fascination that would ultimately lead him to become one of our most distinguished evolutionary biologists.

But having graduated from Magdalene College, Cambridge with a disappointing Second Class degree in Natural Sciences, David Lack was at a loose end. So when the opportunity came up for the post at Dartington, he appears to have jumped at the chance. What the rather shy, strait-laced young man made of the reality of the Elmhirsts' progressive vision for the school – described by one inmate, the educationalist Michael Young, as 'a magnet for devotees of naked bodies and cabbage juice' – is hard to imagine. Nor do we know how he dealt with the artist Lucian Freud, one of his pupils. But he did find a warm welcome for his pacifism, a controversial standpoint at a time when growing militarism in Europe was being fuelled by Hitler's rapid rise to power.

Lack also appreciated the school's rural setting, amidst 1,200 acres of woodland and meadows, awash with birds and other wildlife. And in January 1935, just over a year after he had arrived at Dartington, he began an intensive field study of a population of robins on a 20-acre site within the grounds. This was partly to assuage his own eagerness to embark on proper zoological studies, but also to find something to occupy the minds of his young pupils, who were encouraged to learn outdoors. From this early impulse to find out more about birds, Lack would go on to develop a distinguished scientific career – indeed, he has been described as 'the Father of Evolutionary Ecology'. But it all began at Dartington.

*   *   *   *   *   *

So I am here to see the place that allowed David Lack to embark on what would become one of the most famous ornithological projects ever undertaken; and arguably the one that set the standard for all future field observations of a single species in such intensive detail.

My first problem, though, is the weather: it has been raining all day, and only now, as the downpour begins to ease, are a few birds beginning to emerge into view. I can hear the high-pitched calls of long-tailed tits, eager to stay in touch with one another as they head along hedgerows like a troop of flying lollipops. On the large, open lawns, pied wagtails hunt for insects – of which, thanks to the mild weather, there are plenty. The leaves are, despite the lateness of the autumn season, only just on the turn, and later on I even see a red admiral, probably the last butterfly of the year, for it is almost November, and the clocks go back this weekend, signalling the coming of winter. But so far, even though I can hear plenty of robins singing in the distance, not a single one has shown itself.

My companion on this visit, Kevin, lives just down the road, and knows Dartington well. He points out the extraordinary range of exotic, non-native trees, including gingkos, a huge mulberry, and a tall, broad swamp cypress which, he tells me, taps into an underground aquifer beneath the quadrangle in which it proudly sits. A row of enormous sweet chestnuts, their fruit fallen over the ground, is a good place to take shelter from the drizzle. Then yet another singing robin reminds me why we are here, and yet as we walk around the grounds they appear resolutely determined not to show themselves.

With its mild climate and plethora of trees, this place still supports enough robins for me to realise that, for the young schoolmaster, this must have presented a wonderful opportunity for detailed study of a single species. Over the course of several years, he made some extraordinary discoveries about our most familiar bird: how they defend their territory; that both males and females regularly sing during the autumn and winter; and that some robins do indeed migrate.

He also began to develop the way of thinking that marked him out as a truly original scientist. For the first time, he started to understand the way that natural selection within a population drives the evolution not of the species as a whole, or the group, but individuals. At the time this was a radical idea, but through his post-war career as a distinguished academic ornithologist, specialising in the population ecology of birds, Lack lived to see it embraced as mainstream thinking.

That this all began with the robin is in some ways pure coincidence. When he began his studies, of course, in the depths of winter, robins were more conspicuous than other small birds – but he might have chosen the equally ubiquitous wren (which was later the subject of a monograph by a Cambridge vicar, Edward Armstrong). But I am glad Lack chose the robin – and as we are about to leave the grounds of Dartington Hall for the last time, one does at last briefly appear, before plunging back into a dense laurel hedge.

When it comes to popular scientific writing, few if any books can rival *The Life of the Robin*. Published in 1943, at the height of the Second World War, it ran to five editions, including a popular Pelican paperback, and was read not only by professional scientists and students of biology, but also by many non-specialists. After helping to develop radar systems during the Second World War, Lack went on to have a distinguished academic career as Director of the Edward Grey Institute of Field Ornithology at the University of Oxford. But although he published many other popular and academic books, his lasting fame arose from those early studies of this common and familiar bird.

David Lack died in 1973, at the early age of 62. The many tributes and obituaries focused mainly on his immense contribution to mainstream science. But they also noted that, by writing *The Life of the Robin*, he had inspired so many ordinary observers to take a closer look at birds – something we continue to do to this day.

And when the short days
    Begin to be cold
Robin redbreast will come home to thee
    And be very bold.

Robert Crowley, 'Of Flatterers', 1550

NOVEMBER

The British would no more eat a robin than they would chew off their own thumb, but this was not always the case. Writing towards the end of Queen Elizabeth I's reign, the naturalist and physician Thomas Muffet (father of 'Little Miss Muffet', from the eponymous nursery rhyme), observed: 'Robin-red-breast is esteemed a good and light meat.'

Our cousins across the Channel agreed. In 1817, the zoologist Baron Georges Cuvier wrote that 'the redbreasts are... very much sought after... and their flesh acquires an excellent fat, which renders it a very delicate meat'. And one French recipe noted that 'this amiable little songster is eaten roasted with bread crumbs', which only proves that a Frenchman would eat his shirt if you cooked it for long enough in a cream-and-white-wine sauce.

It may be hard to imagine how such a small bird could provide anything more than an *amuse-bouche*. But, as the Victorian explorer and naturalist Charles Waterton discovered when he found robins for sale in a market in Rome, the secret was to consume them in vast quantities:

'Is it possible,' I asked the vendor, 'that you can kill and eat these pretty songsters?'

'Yes,' said he with a grin, 'and if you will take a dozen of them home for your dinner today, you will come back for two dozen tomorrow.'

By that time the British had, it seems, ended what we would consider the barbaric practice of eating robins. They did, however, continue to feast on other songbirds for many years afterwards – as late as 1861, Mrs Beeton was not averse to including a recipe for lark pie in her *Book of Household Management*.

One reason why robins were so widely eaten was that they were both common and – because of their legendary tameness – very easy to catch. As early as 1674, in his four-part guide *The Gentleman's Recreation* – which covered 'Hunting, Hawking, Fowling, Fishing' – the Restoration writer Nicholas Cox stated that, 'The way of taking a Robin-red-breast is so easie and common, that every Boy knows how to take him in a Pitfall [trap]...'

Little over a century later, in 1792, the French ornithologist Buffon also noted the ease of trapping the robin: 'It is always the first bird that is caught by the decoy.' Even David Lack – who knew a thing or two about catching robins – was rather contemptuous of their naivety:

In winter robins are easy to trap, for they soon come down to investigate any strange object in their territory. If they were human they would be described as curious, but it is difficult to know just what this means in a bird's mind.

Most famously of all, in William Blake's poem 'Auguries of Innocence', written in the early years of the nineteenth century (though not published until 1863, long after his death), he penned the immortal lines:

A Robin Redbreast in a Cage

Puts all Heaven in a Rage.

Often used as a campaign slogan against the enslavement of people, as well as nature, Blake's couplet perfectly captures the indignation we feel when we see a wild bird confined against its will.

It is often said that robins on the continent are far less tame and confiding than their British cousins. Lack suggested that there were good reasons for this: the properties of our European neighbours do not usually have gardens, so continental birds tend to either stay put in the woods for the winter or head south. He also pointed out that in southern Europe – especially Spain, Italy, Cyprus and Malta – robins are, like other songbirds, regularly shot for 'sport', or trapped for the pot. But the writings of French authors such as Cuvier and Buffon suggest that even if continental robins were not quite as tame as their counterparts on our side of the Channel, they were just as easy to catch.

Another reason for the tameness of British robins is the continued presence of wild boars on mainland Europe. So while continental robins followed wild boars around in order to obtain the invertebrates produced when their tusks turned over the soil, in Britain – with boars hunted to extinction during the medieval period – they followed people instead. Why other small birds such as thrushes, blackbirds and dunnocks did not become so tame is a bit of a puzzle: it may go back to the robin's large eyes. In dark forests, at dawn and dusk when boar mainly feed, I suspect the robin was the only forest bird able to see the prey exposed by their foraging.

As all gardeners know, as soon as you take out your spade and begin digging, a robin will miraculously appear and begin to feed. This habit was noted as early as the 1820s by John Clare in his poem 'Home Pictures in May':

> And sweet the robin spring's young luxury shares
> Tuteling its song in feathery gooseberry tree
> While watching worms the gardener's spade unbars...

Another of Clare's poems, 'The Woodman', suggests that this relationship began long before the rise of gardening:

> The robin, tamest of the feather'd race
> Soon as he hears the woodman...
> Around his old companions fearless hops
> And there for hours in pleasd attention stops...

Our enduring fascination with this wild bird's tameness goes all the way back to the story of St Serf in the sixth century. Periodically through history, others have tried to tame a robin, usually by offering it food. One famous 'robin-tamer' was the early-twentieth-century Liberal politician and statesman Sir Edward Grey, the man who poignantly declared, on the eve of the First World War, 'The lamps are going out all over Europe, we shall not see them lit again in our life-time.'

Foreign Secretary from 1905 to 1916 – the longest continuous period served by anyone in that office – Grey found respite from the pressures of his job by watching birds. After he retired, in 1927, he published a slim volume, *The Charm of Birds*, which became an unexpected bestseller and remains a classic of early nature writing.

When he could, Grey would spend time either at his home near Itchen in Hampshire, or on his large country estate at Fallodon, in Northumberland. To amuse himself, he would try to hand-tame the local robins – and usually succeed. With practice, he found, he could do so remarkably easily:

The bird is first attracted by crumbs of bread thrown onto the ground; then a mealworm is thrown to it; then a box… is placed open on the ground with mealworms in it. When the bird has become used to this, the next step is to kneel down and place the back of one hand flat upon the ground, with the box open on the upturned palm, and the fingers projecting beyond the box. This is the most difficult stage, but robins will risk their lives for mealworms, and the bird will soon face the fingers and stand on them. The final stage, that of getting the bird to come on to the hand when raised above the ground is easy.

This works better in winter, Grey went on to explain, when the robin is likely to be more desperate for food:

The whole process may be a matter of only two or three days in hard weather, when birds are hungry; and when once it has been accomplished the robin does not lose its tameness: confidence has been established and does not diminish when weather becomes mild and food plentiful.

Like many acute observers, Grey even learned to recognise individual robins by tiny distinguishing features on their plumage. One of the very first he managed to tame had a distinctive white feather on his right wing, making him easy to pick out from the rest. Oddly, this never disappeared, even when the bird moulted. 'White Feather' survived longer than most robins: Grey first encountered him in the winter of 1921-22, and followed his life cycle all the way through the following three years, until their last meeting, on New Year's Eve 1924:

On the last day of the year… he came to me at the usual spot; after that I never saw him again, and his place was taken by another robin. I searched in the hope that White Feather might only have been driven farther west; but there was no sign, and I fear that there had been combat to the death.

The author and naturalist Seton Gordon took a memorable photograph of Grey with one of these tame robins perched jauntily on his hat. Grey's affection for the robin was enhanced by the fact that, even before *The Charm of Birds* was published, he was rapidly losing his sight. So the song of the robin – especially in autumn and winter, when few if any birds would be singing in the grounds of Fallodon – gave him great comfort in his later years.

In another characteristically thoughtful passage, Grey mused on whether there really is a difference between the robin's spring and autumn songs, or

whether this is a false impression, caused by a change in our own feelings and emotions at these very different times of year:

> In estimating the difference between spring and autumn songs allowance must be made for the human mood... In autumn, when... the sun is getting lower and the days shorter, our own minds are attuned to a minor key, and we find it in the robin's song. On a warm April day, when sap is rising and we are full of anticipation... we judge the robin's song differently... And so I ask, listening to a robin in spring and comparing the impression remembered of the autumn, 'Is it the song or is it I that have changed?'

Almost a century after Sir Edward Grey learned to tame robins, the nature writer and hedgehog-enthusiast Hugh Warwick did the same. Having challenged Andrew Lack – the ornithologist son of David – to prove that robins were equal to his beloved hedgehogs, Hugh tried out a different technique perfected by Andrew's mother (and David's widow) Elizabeth, using cheese instead of mealworms.

To his surprise, after several days of enticing the robin with lumps of best Cheddar, this worked. As he reflected afterwards:

> I might not be able to pet my robin – but there is something very special about the impossibly light bundle of energy that will sometimes spend a few seconds on my hand. I have been lucky enough to be able to share the delight – my wife, children and friends have all had a grin-inducing moment of wildlife connection. For me this is so much more fulfilling than watching the celebrities of the charismatic mega-fauna prancing around in HD on my TV.

But the story wasn't quite over, as Hugh explained:

One morning I was having a snooze in the conservatory when I was woken by a *'cheep, cheep...'* I looked down and the robin was hopping around my feet. I went to the fridge, took the grain of cheese, and as I stood there, feeding the bird, feeling a little bleary, it dawned on me that perhaps I had not trained the robin, it had trained me.

That's something that has probably occurred to every gardener who has ever paused to rest on their spade, and watched a robin snatching a free meal from around their feet.

As autumn gives way to winter, and chill winds sweep across the Atlantic bringing gusty showers to our Somerset garden, I notice the falling-off of the robin's autumn song. Having announced its presence with such a glorious fanfare in early September, it is almost as if the male robin holding a territory outside my bedroom window is losing his enthusiasm; now, I only hear a few desultory phrases as I struggle to awaken from my sleep.

As the world begins to shut down, the days get shorter and the weather gets worse, I feel the need for an injection of nature, so I head out for a walk around my local patch – the wetland reserve and reed-bed on the edge of the Somerset Levels' Avalon Marshes. Here, too, the robins are quieter than before, though I still hear them singing from time to time throughout the month.

One of the reasons robins sing less as the year draws towards a close is that, having established their autumn territories – and maybe even fended off some incomers from Scandinavia – they can relax a little. The other is that with the hours of daylight gradually winding down towards the winter solstice just before Christmas, the need to spend the time finding food becomes more of a priority.

At this time of year, insects are becoming few and far between. That's one of the reasons many hen robins choose to spend the winter either in the milder south and west of Britain, or across the Channel, where insect food is more readily available, and there is less competition with the more dominant males.

In the absence of insects, those robins that stay behind on or near their breeding territory seek out a range of more readily available food. Purple clumps of ivy berries are ideal: these late fruits provide plenty of energy at a time when the earlier fruiting plants, such as hawthorn, are no longer available. But at this time of year robins have to compete with many other birds, including blackbirds, song and mistle thrushes, and two species that come to Britain from the north and east for the winter, fieldfare and redwing. All are larger – though not always feistier – than the little robin.

Robins are also regular visitors to garden bird feeders. However, unlike the more acrobatic tits and finches, they usually stay away from the feeders and either forage on bird tables or stay down on the ground, picking up seeds dropped from above. But in the past few years I have noticed robins become better at clinging on to hanging feeders, though unlike tits and finches they are not very adept at this, and always look as if they are about to fall off!

A merry Christmas.

The North Wind doth blow
And we shall have Snow
And what will poor Robin do then, poor thing?

Anonymous, sixteenth century

DECEMBER

The first card drops through our letterbox sometime in the first week of December, reminding me that this year I really must try to get my shopping done before Christmas Eve. As I slit open the envelope I am not surprised that the image on the front of the card shows a robin perched on a holly-covered branch, surrounded by snow. It's not the only one: during the next few weeks many of the cards we receive will show one, two or even a whole flock of robins, even though such sociable gatherings would never occur in nature.

Robins are such a ubiquitous image on Christmas cards that most of us probably never stop to wonder why. The reason goes back to the early days of the 'Penny Post', starting in 1840, when a card or letter could be sent for one old penny (roughly equivalent to twenty pence today).

Soon afterwards, the civil servant Sir Henry Cole, who worked as the assistant to the Penny Post's inventor, Rowland Hill, had the bright idea of commissioning special cards, which could be sent to friends and family using the new service. Initially, for Christmas 1843, he printed just over 2,000 cards, sold for a shilling (5p, equivalent to about £2 in today's money). A hundred and fifty or so years later, Britons now annually send almost one billion Christmas cards – more than a dozen each for every man, woman and child in the country – with a total value of £200 million.

So how did robins come to feature on this new and soon-to-be-popular product? One plausible explanation is, of course, that robins are still singing throughout the festive season, and also habitually come to our back doorsteps at this time of year for food. This combination of tameness and year-round singing has always endeared the robin to us, so what could be more natural than to celebrate our connection with this little bird by including it on our Christmas cards?

But although that may have started the tradition, the link between robins and Christmas had a major boost in Victorian times – and all because of a fortunate coincidence. The postmen of Victorian England happened to wear bright red uniforms, and so were nicknamed 'Robins'. In *Framley Parsonage*, the 1861 novel written by Anthony Trollope (himself a senior Post Office employee), the kindly cook Jemima invites the visiting postman indoors on a cold winter's day: 'Come in, Robin postman, and warm theeself awhile.'

In those days, as Christmas approached, people would eagerly await the arrival of the postman, and as a result this tableau was chosen as an illustration by the early greetings card artists. It was a short step to swap the postman in his red uniform for an actual robin, which was often depicted holding the card in its beak. The Victorians even sent cards featuring a dead robin, supposedly (though it's hard to imagine how!) a symbol of good luck. And even though the colour of the uniforms worn by postmen and -women changed long ago, we still have red Royal Mail vans and post boxes, a nod to the service's original branding.

The link between robins and Christmas may, however, have its origins in the more distant past. One myth suggests that the robin originally got its red breast when it fanned the flames of a fire in the stable to warm baby Jesus, getting singed in the process. Another folk tale has the robin relieving the lost souls in Purgatory by fetching water for them, and again getting burned.

As Mark Cocker points out in *Birds Britannica*, 'There may even be a dash of paganism in our choice of the robin as the bird of Christmas. Like the holly wreath with its bright-red berries, it provides a splash of living colour in a dead world.'

Aside from this myth and legend, what is the *real* robin doing at this time of year? Well, that partly depends on the prevailing weather conditions. If the south-westerly Atlantic airstream is dominant, bringing bands of low pressure, cloud and rain across the British Isles, then for most robins it is business as usual. As autumn gradually slides into winter, there are still plenty of berries on the hedgerows, and worms and grubs in the fields and gardens, for them to eat.

But if winter has come early, with high-pressure systems bringing streams of Arctic air down from the far north, along with heavy falls of snow, then things are very different. Like all small birds, the robin needs to switch from maintenance mode to a fight for survival, in which every moment of every day is crucial.

As we saw at the start of the year, finding food is the key; and so as the nights draw in even further towards the winter solstice, when there is twice as much darkness as daylight, robins must spend more or less every waking hour feeding or looking for food. They are of course helped by their large, beady eyes, which enable them to begin feeding significantly earlier in the day, and stop later, than other songbirds.

Like many other species, robins also significantly change their diet in the winter months. The insects that were so abundant during the spring and summer, and on which they fed their chicks, are now either absent or hard to find. So robins turn to berries – especially the later-fruiting ivy – or follow gardeners around as they turn over the soil in preparation for planting, to grab a juicy worm or two. And, of course, they come to our bird feeding-stations: usually perching on bird tables or feeding on spilt seed below.

Robins have other survival techniques to cope with cold weather and lack of food: like other small birds they have taken advantage of the glut of food earlier in the autumn to fatten themselves up, their weight rising from an average of around 18 grams to between 22 and 25 grams – almost an ounce. People often think that robins are plumper in winter, and up to a point they are, but that is also because they have fluffed up their feathers to trap a layer of air beneath, to keep warm.

Despite their rather anti-social behaviour most of the time, robins can be forced by prolonged spells of hard weather to change their habits and live more communally. For example, it was long assumed that, unlike many other songbird species such as pied wagtails and long-tailed tits, which roost together to keep warm and safe against predators, robins always remained solitary, even on the coldest winter nights. Indeed, as recently as 1971 a leading Israeli scientist, Amotz Zahavi, could confidently state that 'solitary feeders like the robin… do not use communal roosts.'

But around the same time, scientists in Aberdeen who were catching and ringing blackbirds at night stumbled across several robin roosts in and around the city, each used by up to fifty different birds. Few have been discovered since, and one theory is that these robins were winter visitors from the continent, rather than local birds, which might explain this unusual occurrence.

David Lack also noted several instances where robins will change their behaviour even more radically: deliberately entering people's homes in harsh winter weather – not simply for an hour or two, but in one instance, in Devon during the long, hard winter of 1880-81, for two whole weeks.

On milder days, some robins, especially males, can still spare the time to sing; indeed, given that the purpose of singing in winter – for both males and females – is to defend their territory and food supply against incomers, one could argue that they cannot afford *not* to. There may even be another motive to their singing: as David Lack observed at Dartington, some robins even paired up as early as the middle of December, though most waited until the more traditional time of February to do so.

That is, of course, if they can survive that long. J.P. Burkitt's robin may have lived to the advanced age of eleven years old, but the majority of robins die before they reach their first birthday, and almost all perish before their second.

Robins die in many different ways. We know this both from anecdotal evidence and that provided by the BTO's ringing scheme, which is now more than a century old, having begun in 1909. That year ornithologists ringed just forty-one robins, whereas nowadays more than 20,000 a year are ringed, the vast majority as adults or juveniles rather than nestlings. Since the scheme began, a grand total of just over one million robins have been ringed and, although as with all songbirds the number of ringed birds found dead is very low, this is still enough to give us some idea of the different causes of death.

Chris Mead, in his 1984 book *Robins*, noted that of the British-ringed robins recovered dead, almost one in four had been killed by cats, while one in ten were the victims of collisions with road vehicles. This would not have surprised Max Nicholson, who as long ago as 1951 noted that:

From a robin's standpoint the British people seem to have only two serious faults – their addiction to rushing through robin territories in heavy vehicles without warning, and their inexplicable passion for deliberately infesting their neighbourhoods with cats.

However, as Mead pointed out, birds that fall victim to cats or cars are far more likely to be found by a member of the public, so we should perhaps treat these figures with some scepticism. After all, those that die quietly beneath a bush or in dense undergrowth are very unlikely to be discovered.

Other causes – each of which was responsible for less than five per cent of all deaths – included being taken by an owl or sparrowhawk, drowning in a water container, hitting glass windows or doors, being caught in traps set for other species of bird or mammal (including in one case a mousetrap, lured by a piece of cheese), or simply 'cold weather'. But many robins probably die from a combination of old age and lack of food, at some point during their first or second winter.

Yet we can still be sure of one thing: any robin that starts the winter alive and well has a less-than-even chance of surviving until the following spring – a sobering thought for those of us attached to 'our' garden robin. David Lack was the first serious scientist to attempt to measure the death rate of robins, doing so from one August to the next, as this gave a better indication of how long the youngsters born each spring and early summer survive.

He came up with the figure of sixty-two out of every hundred adults dying from year to year. This was immediately disputed by his fellow ornithologists, who thought it far too high, yet it has since proved to be remarkably accurate. Lack also calculated how many youngsters each pair of robins needs to produce that, when balanced with the even higher mortality

rate for young robins, would keep numbers stable. This figure – roughly six fledglings per pair from one or two broods – is again very close to what we still see in robin populations. This brings us to the 64,000-dollar question: is Britain's robin population rising or falling? Bearing in mind that the majority of songbirds are currently in decline, it might surprise you to learn that robins are bucking the trend.

From the mid-1960s to the mid-1980s, Britain's robin population saw a slow but steady fall, probably because that period saw a run of colder-than-average winters. But since the mid-1980s, the trend has been steadily upwards, so that now the robin has nudged ahead of its closest rivals, the blackbird and chaffinch, to become Britain's second commonest bird (behind the wren), with roughly six million pairs in the UK. This is the result of increased breeding productivity, with fewer nests failing at the egg or chick stage, and also perhaps helped by the onset of global warming, which has allowed robins to begin nesting, on average, a week earlier than in the 1960s.

Robins seem to be prospering even more in England than Scotland, Wales or Northern Ireland, though they are increasing everywhere. The latest BTO Bird Atlas, a nationwide survey of Britain's birds carried out at the end of the first decade of the twenty-first century, revealed that robins were present in 94% of 10-km squares, being absent only from the remotest and highest parts of the Scottish Highlands and Islands. That figure holds true throughout the year, as befits this largely sedentary bird.

Robins are also doing better in some habitats than others. Although they are declining slightly in woodland and especially in the uplands, they are booming in man-made habitats: notably urban and suburban parks and gardens. Since 1995, members of the BTO's Garden BirdWatch scheme have closely monitored the numbers and frequency of birds in our gardens. Not surprisingly, the robin regularly features towards the top of the 'league table', hovering between second place in autumn and winter and fourth in spring and summer.

So the good news is that the robin is doing rather well, at a time when many of our favourite birds with an equally important role to play in our culture, such as the skylark and nightingale, are in serious decline. And although poets may prefer the latter two species, in popular culture the robin reigns supreme. Not only has it been confirmed as the runaway winner of the title of Britain's Favourite Bird, it has now also been given the dubious accolade of the starring role in a Christmas TV advert.

In 2016, the upmarket supermarket chain Waitrose took a leaf out of its big brother John Lewis's book, by producing a heart-rendingly sentimental seasonal advert set to music. The ninety-second mini-epic featured a (computer-generated) robin migrating from the frozen north, across icy wastes, rough seas and snowy landscapes, to end up on a bird table in an English garden.

Along the way it encountered every possible hazard: heavy rain, attack by a merlin, crashing into a lighthouse, falling into the raging sea (from where it was rescued by a kindly fisherman, and then released), before it finally arrived, to feast on a mince pie, accompanied by a second robin. The robin's journey was intercut with footage of a remarkably ornithologically aware young girl, who somehow knew that the robin was on its way. The Twitter hashtag was #HomeForChristmas, designed to wring every last drop of emotion out of the story.

It seems rather churlish to point out that robins migrate in autumn, not winter; and by night, not day; that merlins do not hunt robins in woods; that any robin falling into the North Sea would surely drown; or that, when it tried to feed, the resident robin would have either chased it away or fought it to the death. Ornithological accuracy was, apparently, irrelevant, yet even the toughest viewer could hardly fail to be moved by this stirring tale of one little bird triumphing against the odds. As one critic admitted, 'I absolutely lose it. Genuine tears, people. Over two tiny robins eating a pie. I am a wreck.'

By mid-November, a full six weeks before Christmas Day, this advert had already gained more than one-and-a-half million views on YouTube. By the time the nation's children were unwrapping their presents on Christmas morning, presumably before tucking into a free-range Waitrose turkey with all the trimmings, it had achieved well over three million hits. There was even a book of the advert, and an interactive game based on it.

The advert's runaway success on social media simply confirms the central place that robins hold in our lives and culture, even today. As author and self-styled 'bad birdwatcher' Simon Barnes has pointed out, this is surely due to their unique combination of tameness, striking appearance and winter song:

> In the darkest times they will give us a sweet song... They will also flaunt themselves, flashing the hot coal of their breasts at rivals, affirming life and bringing warmth to the bleakest day. At the winter solstice we celebrate the darkest time of year. It's all about the hope that lies ahead as the year turns. As the robins remind us every day.

Back in the garden, on New Year's Eve, a light fall of snow has covered the ground like a thin layer of icing sugar. Under the bushes, out of sight of all but the most assiduous observer, lies a small, stiff corpse. Already sinking into the snow, it is lying on its back, the feet protruding into the air as if grasping for life, while the orange-red breast shines in the fading afternoon light.

A robin: one of the unlucky ones – a youngster hatched earlier in the year that did manage to survive the perils of leaving the nest and embarking on its adult life. But the recent spell of cold weather has made it much harder to find food, and, as one of the less experienced, and less dominant, females, she simply could not win the race to find enough energy to survive. Her weight gradually dropped, and when she died she tipped the scales at just 12 grams – less than half an ounce – well below the weight at which a robin is able to survive.

During the night, as the temperature drops and the snow continues to fall, the corpse will first freeze and then disappear under a layer of white. A fitting shroud for a bird so associated with the dead of winter.

But for every death there is a rebirth, and just as dawn breaks tomorrow, one of this bird's siblings will wake, fluff out its feathers against the cold, and flit up to the top of the same bush. Then, as the sun rises for the first time in the New Year, he will open his beak and begin to sing.

Another year, with all that it will bring, for both the robins and us.

ACKNOWLEDGEMENTS

As always, I'd like to thank the team at Square Peg (imprint of Penguin Random House): the wonderful Rosemary Davidson, who commissioned the book in the first place; Susannah Otter, Nick Skidmore, Madeleine Hartley and Rowan Yapp in Editorial; Naomi Mantin in Publicity; proofreader Laura Evans; and the talented designers and production team, including picture researcher Lily Richards, led by Design Director Suzanne Dean, who always make my books look so good.

During the writing of the book I was given helpful advice by Hein van Grouw at the Natural History Museum, naturalist John Walters, birder Warren Collum, Paul Stancliffe at the BTO, and my old school friend and birding companion Daniel Osorio. My friends Kevin and Donna Cox kindly allowed me to use their home as a writing retreat, while Kevin also accompanied me on my visit to Dartington Hall. Another dear friend, Graham Coster, edited the book with his usual blend of finesse, skill and perception, while my agent

Broo Doherty was as always a great support. David Lindo inspired me with his campaign to find Britain's Favourite Bird.

Finally, no book on the robin could fail to acknowledge a giant of twenti-eth-century ornithology, David Lack. As a young schoolmaster in Devon he began his study of this common and familiar species, making extraordinary discoveries about its lifecycle. The resulting book, *The Life of the Robin*, re-mains an inspiration; as does *Redbreast*, a collection of writings on the robin compiled by David's son Andrew. Both books are essential reading for any-one interested in the biological and cultural history of this delightful bird.

STEPHEN MOSS

Mark, Somerset
April 2017

BIBLIOGRAPHY

Anderson, Ted R., *The Life of David Lack*. Oxford: **Oxford University Press**, 2013

Clement, Peter and Rose, Chris, *Robins and Chats*. London: **Christopher Helm**, 2015

Cocker, Mark and Mabey, Richard, *Birds Britannica*. London: **Chatto & Windus**, 2005

Lack, Andrew, *Redbreast: The Robin in Life and Literature*. Pulborough: **SMH Books**, 2008

Lack, David, *The Life of the Robin*. Worcester and London: **H.F. & G. Witherby**, 1943

Mead, Chris, *Robins*. London: **Whittet Books**, 1984

Read, Mike, King, Martin and Allsop, Jake, *The Robin*. London: **Blandford**, 1992

Taylor, Marianne, *Robins*. London: **Bloomsbury**, 2015

LIST OF ILLUSTRATIONS

Endpapers from *Birds with their Nests and Eggs Vol. I* by Arthur G. Butler (Brumby & Clarke Ltd, 1896). With thanks to the London Library

p.8 A robin singing (*British Library, London, UK / © British Library Board / Bridgeman Images*)

p.28 Robin Redbreast, border detail from the Sherborne Missal, c.1400 (manuscript) (*British Library, London, UK / © British Library Board*)

p.34 Romantic greetings card in the form of a fan (© *The David Pearson Collection/Mary Evans Picture Library*)

p.39 Robin Red-Breast (chromolitho) (*Private Collection / © Look and Learn / Rosenberg Collection / Bridgeman Images*)

p.44 Courtship display sketch from *Birds and Their Young* by T.A. Coward (Gay & Hancock Ltd, 1923) With thanks to the London Library

p.50 *Primrose and Robin* by John William Wainwright (*Royal Albert Memorial Museum, Exeter, Devon, UK / Bridgeman Images*) p.60 Diagram of robin territories from *The British Bird Book Vol. I*, ed. by F.B. Kirkman (T.C. & E.C. Jack, 1911) With thanks to the London Library

p.63 *Robin, Building the Nest* by Hector Giacomelli (*Private Collection / © Look and Learn / Bridgeman Images*)

p.68 Diagram of birds' eggs from *Birds with their Nests and Eggs Vol. I* by Arthur G. Butler (Brumby & Clarke Ltd, 1896) With thanks to the London Library

p.75 *Robin, Feeding the Young* by Hector Giacomelli (*Private Collection / © Look and Learn / Bridgeman Images*)

p.78 Robin's nest in an old hat from *The British Bird Book Vol. I*, ed. by F.B. Kirkman (T.C. & E.C. Jack, 1911) With thanks to the London Library

p.82 Robin in a nesting box on a greetings card (© *The David Pearson Collection/Mary Evans Picture Library*)

p.90 Erythacus rubecula (*Natural History Museum, London, UK / Bridgeman Images*)

p.95 Robins feeding chicks from *Birds and Their Young* by T.A. Coward (Gay & Hancock Ltd, 1923) With thanks to the London Library

p.98 Antique Print of a European Robin, 1859 (*Photo © GraphicaArtis / Bridgeman Images*)

p.105 Cock Robin (*Private Collection / © Look and Learn / Bridgeman Images*)

p.111 British and Continental robins from *The Handbook of British Birds Vol. II* by H.F. Witherby, Rev. F.C.R. Jourdain, Norman F. Ticehurst and Bernard W. Tucker (H.F. & G. Witherby Ltd, 1938) With thanks to the London Library

p.114 *Robin* by Joseph Mallord William Turner from *The Farnley Book of Birds*, c.1816 (*Leeds Museums and Galleries (Leeds Art Gallery) U.K. / Bridgeman Images*)

p.119 *A Robin Perched on a Mossy Stone* by John James Audubon (*University of Liverpool Art Gallery & Collections, UK / Bridgeman Images*)

PL. I.

FIGS. 1— 4 MISSEL THRUSH.
5- 9 SONG THRUSH.
10 17 BLACKBIRD.

FIGS. 18—19 RING OUZEL.
20 WHEATEAR.
21 22 WHINCHAT.
23 STONECHAT.

FIGS. 24 REDSTART
25- 28 REDBREAST
29 31 NIGHTINGALE.